I0438736

2012 NATIONAL EXPORT STRATEGY

Powering the National Export Initiative: Year 3

United States of America
Trade Promotion Coordinating Committee
Washington, D.C.
December 2012

1211-11-08

Letter From Secretary Blank

Dear Mr. President and Mr. Speaker:

With unprecedented leadership from President Obama and cooperation across the Federal Government on the National Export Initiative (NEI), it is my great privilege to present the 2012 National Export Strategy of the Trade Promotion Coordinating Committee (TPCC).

The past three years have seen rapid growth in U.S. exports — continuing progress toward achieving President Obama's goal of doubling exports by the end of 2014. In 2011, U.S. goods and services exports reached a record $2.1 trillion. These historic 2011 U.S. export figures represented an increase of 33 percent over the level of U.S. exports in 2009. In 2012, we are on track to again achieve record exports, with U.S. goods and services exports in the first nine months of 2012 totaling a record $1.6 trillion, up by $76.5 billion from the same period of 2011. Importantly, the benefits of exporting are being shared more broadly. A record 293,000 U.S. companies exported in 2010 (latest available data) —16,500 more than in 2009. Small businesses—the country's biggest job creators and the primary customers of Federal export assistance—continued to steadily grow their share of overall U.S. exports to 34 percent in 2010 (latest available data), up from 27 percent in 2002. The end result is employment for Americans, with exports supporting 1.2 million more jobs in 2011 than in 2009.

Thanks to America's strong reputation for innovation, quality, and safety, U.S. goods and services remain the gold standard. For its part, the Federal Government is committed to helping U.S. businesses build things here and sell them everywhere, with the NEI complementing other Administration initiatives on advanced manufacturing, innovation, and protection of intellectual property. In Chapter 1, we highlight the TPCC agencies' achievements to date and their progress on special initiatives highlighted in the 2011 report, including the Metropolitan Export Initiative, the enactment of legislation approving the Korea, Colombia, and Panama Free Trade Agreements, and the staffing of a new Interagency Trade Enforcement Center.

But this is no time to rest, as the United States faces a challenging period ahead. The International Monetary Fund's October 2012 World Economic Outlook reported that world economic growth slowed in the first half of 2012, with negative growth in Europe and slower growth in China and India. Therefore, the TPCC agencies have redoubled their efforts. Chapter 2 is devoted to small businesses and the Export Promotion Cabinet's aggressive plan for maximizing the effectiveness of Federal programs by increasing the national base of small business exporters, expanding the reach of Federal export assistance and counseling for small businesses, and ensuring better delivery of export services domestically and overseas. Chapter 3 looks over the horizon at strategic initiatives as global consumption shifts to emerging markets and as foreign competition for these markets intensifies. Strategies include coordination on infrastructure projects, a strengthened focus on the Asia-Pacific region, a strategy for increased commercial engagement with Africa, and promotion of the SelectUSA program to attract and retain investment in the United States.

More than ever, the United States is distinguished by the innovation, entrepreneurial spirit, and hard work of Americans throughout our country. We look forward to working with you to ensure that these great American strengths translate into a boom in U.S. exports and the new jobs and prosperity that those exports create, so we can continue the momentum of 33 straight months of job growth in America with a 5.6 million increase in private sector employment.

Sincerely,

Dr. Rebecca Blank
Acting Secretary of Commerce and Chair of the
Trade Promotion Coordinating Committee

Table of Contents

Introduction:
Obama Administration's
Commitment To Export Growth....... 1

The President Strengthens the NEI Mandate.............. 1
Overview of the 2012 National Export Strategy 2

Chapter 1: NEI Accomplishments to Date and Follow-up on Priority Initiatives.. 4

Economic Snapshot: U.S. Exports, Jobs Supported, and Number of Businesses Exporting All See Gains .. 4
NEI Success Resulting from More Effective Federal Trade Programs 5
Improved Advocacy and Trade Promotion Programs 5
Greater Access to Export Financing 6
Successful Removal of Trade Barriers 6
Stronger Enforcement of Trade Rules 8
Promotion of Stronger, More Sustainable, and More Balanced Growth 12

Implementation of Key 2011 National Export Strategy Priorities 12
Collaboration with States and Metropolitan Areas 12
Export.gov Next Generation 13
Congressional Approval of Korea, Colombia, and Panama Trade Agreements 14
Improvement of the U.S. Supply Chain Infrastructure 14
Increased Administration Focus on Travel and Tourism's Potential 16

Chapter 2: The EPC's Plan for Maximizing the Effectiveness of Federal Programs............................ 18

Economic Snapshot: U.S. Small Businesses Power More of America's Exports. 18
Export Promotion Cabinet (EPC) Priorities for Maximizing the Effectiveness of Federal Programs.. 19
Goal 1: Increase the National Base of Small Business Exporters ... 20
Goal 2: Make It Easier for U.S. Businesses to Access Federal Export Assistance 21
Goal 3: Improve Strategic Delivery of Federal Export Assistance 21

Chapter 3: Looking Over the Horizon in a Rapidly Changing Global Marketplace 23

Economic Snapshot: Robust Emerging Market Growth and Strong Foreign Competition Define a Global Marketplace Full of Both Opportunities and Challenges 23
Global Market Trends 23
Foreign Competition 23
Staying Ahead of the Curve: U.S. Government Strategies 25
Improve the Targeting of Infrastructure Projects 25
Strengthen Asia-Pacific Policy and Promotion Efforts 25
Strengthen Africa Commercial Engagement 26
Attract and Retain More Investment with SelectUSA 26
The Administration's FY 2013 Trade Promotion Budget 28

Chapter 4: NEI Progress Metrics 29

Economic Snapshot: Macroeconomic Metrics Show Steady Progress 29
NEI Progress Metrics 29
Strengthen Advocacy and Export Promotion 29
Provide Greater Access to Export Financing 34
Reduce Trade Barriers and Enforce Trade Rules 36

Appendix A: Tracking Progress on the September 2010 NEI Recommendations........................... 39

NEI Recommendations Update 39
Priority 1: Exports by SMEs 40
Priority 2: Federal Export Assistance 43
Priority 3: Trade Missions 46
Priority 4: Commercial Advocacy 47
Priority 5: Increasing Export Financing 48
Priority 6: Macroeconomic Rebalancing 49
Priority 7: Reducing Barriers to Trade 50
Priority 8: Export Promotion of Services 56

Appendix B: Abbreviations List 57

Introduction:
Obama Administration's Commitment To Export Growth

When the President announced the National Export Initiative (NEI) in 2010, with the ambitious goal of doubling U.S. exports over five years, he made clear that boosting U.S. exports was not only a short-term strategy but also a critical component of America's long-term prosperity. The launch of the NEI, as well as the establishment of the Export Promotion Cabinet (EPC), was the first in a series of steps to promote U.S. exports and marshal the full resources of the Federal Government to support U.S. exporters. These efforts have borne considerable fruits. Exports hit record levels in 2011, and this historic progress has ensured America's continued position as the global leader in total exports.

However, with U.S. exports facing headwinds from the economic slowdown in Europe and Asia, the Administration must reinvigorate its efforts to help U.S. businesses, particularly small firms, compete for the 95 percent of the world's customers who live outside the United States. In a rapidly changing global business environment, the mandate of the NEI requires federal agencies to re-think their traditional approaches to export assistance so they can better serve their customers, partners, and stakeholders throughout the United States. In addition, the Department of Commerce has integrated its NEI Office with that of the TPCC Secretariat to create a "whole of government" approach to implementing the NEI.

The President Strengthens the NEI Mandate

Since the last report, the President issued two Memoranda that not only emphasized the need for federal agencies to make it easier for America's small businesses and exporters to access federal assistance but also compelled the EPC to work to maximize the effectiveness of federal programs that promote trade and investment.

In a Memorandum dated October 28, 2011, the President directed agencies to better facilitate access to government export promotion services by doing the following:

> adopting a "No Wrong Door" policy that uses technology to quickly connect businesses to the services and information relevant to them, regardless of which agency's website, call center, or office they go to for help
> …

Additionally, in a Memorandum dated February 17, 2012, the President directed the EPC to develop strategies to better facilitate the Administration's strategic trade and investment objectives:

> [T]he Export Promotion Cabinet shall develop strategies and initiatives in support of my Administration's strategic trade and investment goals and priorities. … The Export Promotion Cabinet shall, in consultation with the TPCC, [ ] evaluate the allocation of Federal Government resources to assist with trade financing, negotiation, enforcement, and promotion, as well as the encouragement of foreign investment in the United States … [and] shall take steps to ensure the most efficient use of its members' domestic and foreign offices and distribution networks including co-locating offices wherever appropriate; [and] cross-training staff to better serve business customers at home and abroad by promoting exports to foreign countries and foreign investment in the United States. …[T]he Export Promotion Cabinet shall work with the National Economic Council to develop and coordinate administrative initiatives to align and enhance programs that enable and support efforts by American businesses, particularly small businesses, to innovate, grow and increase exports.

Overview of the 2012 National Export Strategy

This National Export Strategy Report to Congress (NES) sets forth the steps taken to implement the EPC's comprehensive plan to carry out the goals of the NEI and to support the creation of U.S. jobs through the promotion of U.S. exports. Exports are an increasingly important component of U.S. economic growth, and more and more individual businesses are discovering the competitive advantages and potential for revenue growth of exporting.

Chapter 1

"NEI Accomplishments to Date and Follow-up on Priority Initiatives"—reports on the success story of U.S. exports over the past three years, with exports playing a prominent role in U.S. economic recovery. The response of U.S. companies, workers, and farmers to overseas market opportunities has been impressive. The TPCC agencies' commitment to the NEI and its goals has improved their across-the-board support of U.S. exports, with impressive results in all of the NEI's priority areas, including improved advocacy and trade promotion programs, greater access to trade financing, successful removal of trade barriers, stronger enforcement of trade rules, and promotion of stronger and more balanced global economic growth. The U.S. Government has also followed through on commitments in the 2011 National Export Strategy, including increased collaboration with U.S. cities and states, development of the next generation of the Export.gov web portal, entry into force of new free trade agreements with Korea, Colombia, and Panama, concrete steps to improve U.S. supply chain infrastructure, and a national tourism strategy to boost U.S. services sector exports. In addition, EPC agencies are staffing a new Interagency Trade Enforcement Center to level the playing field and enhance the investigation of unfair trade practices.

Chapter 2

"The EPC's Plan for Maximizing the Effectiveness of Federal Programs"—reports on the EPC's response to the President's strategic directives noted earlier. Led by the President's National Security Staff and National Economic Council, and supported by the TPCC, the U.S. Government has made unprecedented strides toward streamlining and modernizing delivery of U.S. export promotion services. In the first half of 2012, the EPC developed an action plan for a more integrated, strategic, government-wide export promotion effort. With U.S. exports growing, there remains tremendous untapped potential for small businesses to begin to export, to export more, and to expand to new markets. Over the next year, the Federal Government will work toward (1) increasing the national base of small- and medium-sized enterprise exporters by 50,000 by 2017, (2) expanding the reach of federal export assistance and counseling to small businesses, and (3) ensuring better delivery of export promotion services domestically and overseas.

Chapter 3

"Looking Over the Horizon in a Rapidly Changing Global Marketplace"—takes forward planning one step further, ensuring that the Federal Government has strategies for the United States to remain competitive in a rapidly evolving global marketplace. Dramatic changes in regional growth rates between the mature industrial economies and the emerging markets are shifting demand to markets that can be more difficult for U.S. companies to navigate. Foreign governments are also responding to global export opportunities with new and sometimes aggressive export promotion programs and initiatives. A new TPCC Working Group on infrastructure is actively identifying specific markets and projects that could yield increasing exports, and also could better position U.S. industries in key markets. Looking toward the future, the Federal Government is developing long-term strategies and alternative export promotion service delivery models in several rapidly growing markets, including the Asia-Pacific region, which now accounts for 54 percent of global economic activity, and

Africa, which contains 6 of the world's 10 fastest-growing economies. Moreover, because new foreign investment is a key factor in U.S. exports, the SelectUSA program is highlighting the United States as the world's most attractive destination for inward investment.

Chapter 4

"NEI Progress Metrics"—discusses the TPCC's role in gathering and tabulating cross-governmental performance data in key program areas. With several new reporting streams created in 2011, the TPCC can now report year-over-year cross-governmental metrics in most areas. These metrics will continue to be an important management tool for the Federal Government.

Appendix A

"Tracking Progress on the September 2010 NEI Recommendations"—summarizes progress on the original NEI recommendations in the EPC's September 2010 NEI Report to the President. The EPC is committed to ongoing implementation and reevaluation of these recommendations in the NEI's priority areas for government action.

Appendix B

Provides an abbreviations list.

Chapter 1:
NEI Accomplishments to Date and Follow-up on Priority Initiatives

Economic Snapshot: U.S. Exports, Jobs Supported, and Number of Businesses Exporting All See Gains

Though much work remains to be done, the United States is making progress toward President Obama's goal in the National Export Initiative (NEI) of doubling U.S. exports by the end of 2014. Exports remain a bright spot for America, with U.S. goods and services exports in the first nine months of 2012 totaling a record $1.6 trillion, up by $76.5 billion from the same period of 2011. The United States remains on track to exceed 2011's record export total of $2.1 trillion. Higher exports support more jobs: the significant increase in exports since 2009 has helped America create 5.6 million jobs over the past 33 months, and, in 2011, jobs supported by exports increased by 1.2 million over 2009.

In 2011, the United States set records for both goods and services exports at $1.5 trillion and $606.0 billion, respectively, and totaling more than $2.1 trillion—the highest amount on record and the first time U.S. exports have crossed the $2 trillion threshold. The U.S. trade surplus in services was $178.5 billion, and the agricultural commodities surplus was $37.2 billion, the highest amount in recorded U.S. history for both of those sectors.

Record-setting exports are having a major influence on U.S. employment. The $2.1 trillion in U.S. exports of goods and services supported 9.7 million jobs in 2011, an increase of 1.2 million since 2009 (see figure 1).

More U.S. companies are discovering that taking their products to foreign markets improves their bottom line by diversifying sales and improving awareness of global trends and competition. In fact, the latest data from the Census Bureau (see figure 2) indicates that a record more than 293,000 companies exported in 2010, exceeding the pre-financial crisis and previous record of nearly 290,000 set in 2008.

Future economic growth and job creation in America calls for a much greater effort to encourage thousands more small businesses to export. Reaching that goal will require an increase in the number of U.S. companies exporting, the amount of goods and services U.S. companies are exporting, and the number of foreign markets to which U.S. companies are exporting.

NEI Success Resulting from More Effective Federal Trade Programs

Improved Advocacy and Trade Promotion Programs

Positive export numbers are due mostly to the world-class competitiveness of the U.S. private sector—its companies, workers, and farmers. However, the Federal Government's implementation of several key NEI recommendations has substantially contributed to this success.

Since the launch of the NEI in January 2010 through September 2012, the Department of Commerce's International Trade Administration (ITA) has helped more than 15,000 U.S. companies achieve a verified export sale for a total of $184 billion in exports supported. Within that period, ITA's assistance supported 217,800 jobs in 2010 and 429,260 jobs in 2011 (the data required to produce jobs supported numbers for 2012 does not yet exist). Program areas contributing to these business and employment successes include:

- **Advocacy.** The Department of Commerce's Advocacy Center serves to level the playing field on behalf of U.S. companies competing for international government contracts. From January 2010 through September 2012, the Advocacy Center coordinated an inter-agency group in support of the NEI to assist hundreds of businesses win foreign government contracts totaling approximately $111 billion in U.S. export content. By instituting an aggressive new client outreach program, the Advocacy Center has nearly doubled the number of active cases from 340 to 670 during this period and is on track for another record-breaking year in 2012.

- **Export promotion services and events.** The Department of Commerce's U.S. & Foreign Commercial Service (U.S. Commercial Service) supported another $73 billion in exports from January 2010 through September 2012 through export promotion activities. These activities include arranging one-on-one meetings between U.S. exporters and potential foreign buyers, organizing special in-country promotions for individual U.S. exporters, and executing other customized in-country market development work on behalf of U.S. exporters. Trade events include bringing over 1,100 U.S. companies on 135 trade missions to 55 countries, bringing over 35,000 foreign buyers to visit major U.S. trade shows to connect with U.S. companies, and supporting almost 12,500 companies participating in foreign trade shows.

The U.S. Department of Agriculture (USDA) also achieved impressive results in 2011. Agriculture is one of the brightest spots in the U.S. economy, and the American brand of agriculture is surging in popularity worldwide. In 2011, U.S. exports of agricultural products totaled $136 billion, the second highest on record, compared to $115 billion in 2010. U.S. agricultural exports support over one million jobs here at home.

- In 2012, USDA supported U.S. pavilions at 27 international trade shows in 18 countries with 1,013 exhibitors reporting $1.3 billion of estimated 12-month sales. In 2011, exhibitors at USDA supported U.S. pavilions reported $1.1 billion in sales.

- In the first six months of 2012, USDA's export program partners organized 141 reverse trade missions, bringing 1,253 foreign buyers to the United States to meet with U.S. suppliers and leading to reported sales of $2.9 billion. In 2011, USDA reverse trade missions lead to reported sales of $1.3 billion.

- In the first six months of 2012, USDA led 37 different agribusinesses on an agricultural trade mission to China resulting in $1.8 million in sales. In 2011, trade missions to markets such as Peru, Indonesia, Vietnam and Colombia resulted in $15 million in sales.

In support of the NEI, the U.S. Trade and Development Agency (USTDA) launched the International Business Partnership Program (IBPP) to connect international buyers with U.S. manufacturers and service providers through reverse trade missions (i.e., bringing potential foreign buyers to the United States), conferences, and workshops. During FY 2011 and 2012, IBPP connected more than 4,000 foreign buyers to over 3,300 U.S. company representatives.

Greater Access to Export Financing

In FY 2012, the Export-Import Bank of the United States (Ex-Im Bank) was able to increase the extension of financing, primarily through its existing export credit programs, by 46 percent over FY2010 (when the Bank extended $24.5 billion in total authorizations) to $35.8 billion in total authorizations, with $6.1 billion going to small businesses. The programs Ex-Im Bank has launched, such as Global Credit Express, and enhanced, such as the bond product/capital market option, continue to contribute to this total. Ex-Im Bank's total authorizations are supporting an estimated $50 billion in U.S. export sales and approximately 255,000 American jobs in communities across the country.

By the end of 2011, more than 500 Small Business Administration (SBA) private sector lenders had signed up to offer the Export Express program which was made a permanent loan program of the SBA in the Small Business Jobs Act (SBJA) of 2010. Volume under this program increased significantly from $13.5 million in FY 2010 to $35.1 million in FY 2012. Likewise, between FY 2010 and FY 2012, volume under the SBA's Export Working Capital program increased from $120 million to $219.6 million and volume under the International Trade Loan dramatically increased from $2.3 million to $95.8 million, a result of both enhancements made to the programs and the new $5 million maximum loan amount allowed under the SBJA.

In the first six months of 2012, USDA's Export Credit Guarantee Program (GSM-102) facilitated agricultural exports of $2.4 billion. In 2011, GSM-102 facilitated agricultural sales of $4.1 billion, an increase of 28 percent over 2010. GSM-102 provides credit guarantees to encourage financing of commercial exports of U.S. agricultural products, while providing competitive credit terms to buyers.

Successful Removal of Trade Barriers

A critical element of the NEI is to remove key impediments to trade through a variety of strategies, from the negotiation of trade liberalizing agreements and initiatives to the deployment of commercial diplomacy to leverage trade agreements and remove a wide range of non-tariff barriers that impede U.S. market access abroad.

Trans-Pacific Partnership (TPP).

- With respect to trade liberalizing initiatives, the United States and the eight other TPP members agreed in late 2011 on the broad outlines for an ambitious, state-of-the-art TPP agreement that will enhance trade and investment among the TPP countries, promote innovation, increase economic growth and development, and support the creation and retention of jobs in America and around the Asia-Pacific region. This agreement will create significant new opportunities to increase U.S. exports that support higher-paying jobs in the United States. The Asia-Pacific region includes some of the world's most dynamic economies, representing more than 40 percent of global trade. The region is already a key destination for U.S. manufactured goods, agricultural products, and services, accounting in 2011 for more than 60 percent of U.S. goods exports and nearly three-quarters of total U.S. agricultural exports. Canada and Mexico have joined the TPP negotiations as of early October 2012, following the successful conclusion of the domestic procedures of each of the current TPP countries for addition of new participants. The inclusion of Canada and Mexico will generate even further opportunities for U.S. export growth, allow U.S. companies to leverage their existing North American supply chains by exporting goods to other TPP countries, and help fulfill President Obama's pledge to improve the North American Free Trade Agreement.

Asia-Pacific Economic Cooperation forum (APEC).

- The United States continues to be actively engaged in APEC, including by acting as APEC host in 2011, to ensure that APEC remains an organization that is known for producing concrete results and meaningful outcomes. Since 2009, the United States has achieved a number of significant outcomes to further facilitate and liberalize trade in the region. In 2012, APEC Leaders agreed on a list of environmental goods on which, according to their 2011 pledge, they will cut tariffs to 5 percent or less by 2015. This agreement marks the first time that trade negotiators have agreed to tariff cuts on a list of environmental goods, an initiative that will help protect the environment while stimulating trade, jobs, and economic growth. Given that the United States exported $27 billion worth of these products to the APEC region in 2011, of which $1.2 billion worth faced tariffs above 5 percent, this outcome will contribute importantly to the Obama Administration's goal to double exports by the end of 2014.

Other outcomes of note included the APEC Leaders' 2011 commitments to (1) implement policies that will set a model for innovation in the region that is market driven and non-discriminatory, not government directed and protectionist, in recognition of the key role entrepreneurship plays in increasing productivity and ensuring economic growth and (2) take steps by 2013 to strengthen the implementation of good regulatory practices, which will promote in the region greater alignment in regulatory approaches, including alignment to international standards. APEC also has a robust trade facilitation agenda that is highlighted by APEC Leaders' 2010 commitment to improve supply chain performance in the region by reducing the time, cost, and uncertainty of moving goods through the region by 10 percent by 2015. Finally, APEC has agreed to launch new work to further break down barriers, including beginning to address local content requirements that have a significant distortive effect on trade and investment.

Open Skies agreements.

- In the area of international aviation, the Departments of State, Transportation, and Commerce are engaged in ongoing market access negotiations, seeking to establish "Open Skies" agreements and to eliminate restrictive aviation regimes worldwide. Such actions allow the U.S. travel and tourism sector, including U.S. passenger airlines, to make a maximum contribution to overall U.S. exports. Removal of restrictions on market entry and service levels allows U.S. cargo airlines to offer their services in international markets with minimal restrictions and to participate more fully in the transport of increased U.S. exports under the NEI. During 2010, Open Skies agreements were reached with Zambia, Israel, Trinidad and Tobago, Barbados, Colombia, and Brazil. In addition, a second-stage agreement was reached with the European Union (EU) and its Member States. During 2011, Open Skies agreements were reached with Saudi Arabia, Macedonia, St. Kitts and Nevis, and Montenegro. So far in 2012, Open Skies agreements have been reached with Suriname and Sierra Leone.

Bilateral investment treaty (BIT) program.

- The United States is actively seeking to enhance market access and legal protection for U.S. investors and their investments through the U.S. BIT program. In January 2012, the United States–Rwanda BIT entered into force. In April, 2012, the United States announced the completion of the review of its Model BIT, clearing the way to resume discussions with key emerging and other developing economies. Formal BIT negotiations with Mauritius resumed in May 2012, and a BIT negotiating round was held with India in June 2012. BIT negotiations are also ongoing with China. Exploratory discussions on potential BIT negotiations also are currently underway. For example, the United States held exploratory talks with the East African Community and Ghana, respectively, in July and August 2012. The United States launched BIT exploratory discussions with Cambodia in August 2012.

Russia's World Trade Organization (WTO) membership.

- The United States, along with other WTO Members successfully concluded negotiations on the terms for Russia's membership in the WTO, and after nearly two decades of effort, Russia became a WTO Member on August 22, 2012. On November 16, 2012, the House of Representatives passed legislation authorizing the President to end the application of Jackson-Vanik and extend Permanent Normal Trade Relations to Russia. On December 6, the Senate approved identical legislation. This legislation paves the way for the United States and Russia to apply the WTO Agreement between them. When the United States applies the WTO Agreement between the United States and Russia, American exporters will be able to realize the full benefits of Russia's membership in the WTO and will be able to compete on a level playing field in the Russian market with exporters from other WTO Members. Benefits to U.S. companies flowing from Russia's membership in the WTO include better protections for U.S. intellectual property rights, greater certainty for U.S. agriculture and industrial goods exports, and more open markets for U.S. audio-visual services, telecommunications, and financial services providers, as well as giving the Administration better tools to resolve trade issues and enforce U.S. rights under the WTO Agreement.

Trade Agreements Compliance Program.

- With respect to efforts to tackle trade and investment barriers affecting U.S. companies and their ability to gain fair access to foreign markets, the Department of Commerce's Trade Agreements Compliance Program in 2011 initiated 246 trade barrier investigations in 72 countries, with 88 investigations (36 percent) on behalf of small- and medium-sized enterprises (SMEs); it successfully resolved 91 barriers to trade in 45 countries, thereby affecting a broad range of industries. To ensure that implemented trade agreements work for America and that U.S. exporters of manufactured goods, U.S. services, and U.S. investors are realizing their full benefits, the Trade Agreements Compliance Program works to break down discriminatory barriers to market access and proactively monitors and pursues foreign trading partner compliance with trade agreement provisions. The program provides a framework for proactive, on-going monitoring of free trade agreements, investment treaties, and WTO obligations; a process for identifying, investigating, and resolving investment and non-tariff barriers by working with companies and foreign governments to resolve issues through commercial diplomacy; and a strategy for conducting outreach to inform stakeholders of efforts and services in this area. There is no cost to U.S. exporters for the services of the Trade Agreements Compliance Program.

Once a barrier is identified, the Department of Commerce assembles a case team of specialists to investigate the problem and develop a strategy to address it. The team then works with affected companies or industries to establish objectives and to implement agreed-upon action plans to achieve market access and ensure that U.S. trade agreement rights are safeguarded. In taking action, the Department of Commerce teams can gradually escalate trade issues, and, as appropriate, bring the full weight of the U.S. Government to bear in an effort to resolve the issues—leveraging relevant trade agreements, multilateral/WTO fora, free trade agreement negotiations, and other diplomatic means. Where barriers cannot be resolved through commercial diplomacy, they may be referred as appropriate to the Office of the United States Trade Representative (USTR), the Interagency Trade Enforcement Center, and interagency for formal dispute settlement action consideration.

Stronger Enforcement of Trade Rules

Through vigorous enforcement of U.S. trade rights under international trade agreements, the United States ensured that more Americans saw the benefits promised by those pacts. The Administration has doubled the rate of WTO challenges against China compared to the prior Administration and has now established a new trade enforcement unit—the Interagency Trade Enforcement Center—to root out unfair trade practices around the globe. Such vigorous enforcement helps American farmers, ranchers, manufacturers, and service providers remain globally competitive, even in today's difficult economic environment. The United States has been very active in pursuing enforcement of its trade rights under various agreements affecting a variety of sectors and industries:

Winning at the WTO against EU subsidies to Airbus.

- In the largest case ever heard by a WTO panel, the WTO Appellate Body upheld a panel's finding that $18 billion in subsidies conferred on Airbus by the EU and member countries were illegal, hurting the U.S. aerospace industry and its workers with lost sales and the loss of global market share. Thanks to this finding, the jobs of thousands of U.S. aerospace engineers and electricians and related suppliers are more secure. More Americans will have a chance at future jobs as the EU comes into compliance and as U.S. aircraft manufacturers compete on a more level playing field.

Winning the largest-ever decision at the WTO in a dispute with the EU over aircraft subsidies.

- The EU asserted that the United States provided almost $20 billion in subsidies to Boeing, but a WTO panel and the WTO Appellate Body rejected the vast majority of the EU's claims. The Appellate Body found that the value of subsidies provided by the United States was in the range of $3–4 billion, and those subsidies had far fewer distortive effects on the aircraft market than subsidies provided by the EU.

Challenging China's unfair restrictions on access to raw materials.

- Both a WTO panel and the WTO Appellate Body agreed with the United States that Chinese export restraints on a number of industrial raw materials (i.e., bauxite, coke, fluorspar, magnesium, manganese, silicon carbide, silicon metal, yellow phosphorus and zinc) violated China's WTO obligations. These export restraints skew the playing field against the United States in the production and export of processed steel, aluminum and chemical products, and a wide range of further processed products. The export restraints artificially increase world prices for these raw material inputs while artificially lowering input prices for Chinese producers, creating significant advantages for China's producers when competing against U.S. producers both in China's market and other countries' markets. The United States will scrutinize carefully China actions to comply with this important victory.

Challenging China's export restraints on rare earth elements, tungsten, and molybdenum.

- The United States initiated a WTO challenge to China's unfair export restraints on rare earth elements, tungsten, and molybdenum—key inputs in many U.S. manufacturing sectors and American made products, including hybrid car batteries, wind turbines, energy-efficient lighting, steel, advanced electronics, automobiles, petroleum, and chemicals. These restraints appear to be part of a troubling industrial policy aimed at providing substantial competitive advantage for Chinese manufacturers at the expense of foreign manufacturers. As a leading global producer of these materials, its export restraints provide unfair advantages to China's downstream producers and pressure foreign producers to move their operations, jobs, and technologies to China.

Successful challenge of Chinese restrictions on the importation and distribution of films, DVDs, music, books, and other copyright-intensive products.

- In January 2010, the WTO Dispute Settlement Body (DSB) adopted panel and Appellate Body reports finding that Chinese restrictions on the importation and distribution of a wide range of copyright-intensive products violated WTO rules. By April 2011, China had made changes to its legal regime relating to DVDs, music, books, and certain other products. In February 2012, following intensive negotiations, the United States announced a breakthrough bilateral agreement that allows significantly more exports of American blockbuster films to China on more favorable revenue-sharing terms, strengthens opportunities to distribute American films through private enterprises rather than the state film monopoly, and ensures fairer compensation levels when U.S. films are being distributed on terms other than a revenue-sharing basis. This victory will support increases in U.S. exports and jobs. Globally, the United States has long been a net exporter of such copyright-intensive products, enjoying a $12 billion annual trade surplus in connection with films and other audio-visual services alone.

Successful resolution of certain deficiencies in China's legal regime for protecting and enforcing copyrights and trademarks.

- Following a successful challenge brought by the United States, the WTO DSB adopted a panel report finding WTO violations in connection with Chinese restrictions on copyright protection for works that do not meet China's content review standards, and in connection with China's Customs rules allowing for public auction of seized counterfeit goods following removal of the infringing mark. In March 2010, China announced that it had completed all the necessary domestic legislative procedures to implement the recommendations and findings of the DSB.

Successfully defending our right to impose duties under the China Specific Safeguard Mechanism.

- The United States successfully defended its right under U.S. and international law to impose additional duties on disruptive imports of certain passenger and light truck tires from China. Both a WTO panel and the WTO Appellate Body rejected all of China's claims against additional duties imposed by President Obama in September 2009 pursuant to section 421 of the Trade Act of 1974, which implemented the transitional safeguard in China's Protocol of Accession to the WTO. As a result of this win, the additional duties on imports of tires from China, which have helped to restore U.S. tire industry jobs, continued to be assessed an additional duty of 25 percent until September 21, 2012.

Enforcing labor rights under the Dominican Republic-Central America–United States Free Trade Agreement (CAFTA-DR).

- The Administration broke new ground when USTR requested the establishment of an arbitral panel pursuant to CAFTA-DR for Guatemala's apparent failure to effectively enforce its labor laws. This is the first labor case the United States has ever brought under a free trade agreement and reflects the Administration's determination to protect the rights of workers in America and abroad and to provide a level playing field for workers here at home.

Challenging Chinese duties on U.S. exports of grain-oriented electrical steel (GOES), chicken broiler products, and automobiles.

- In three separate cases, the Administration has challenged China's imposition of antidumping and countervailing duties on exports to China of American GOES, chicken broiler products, and automobiles. In the GOES case, a WTO panel upheld U.S. claims that China had failed to abide by its substantive and procedural obligations in imposing the duties. The U.S. challenges to China's duties on chicken broiler products and automobiles are pending. In each of these cases, the United States is fighting to ensure that China does not block U.S. exports by misusing its trade laws and violating its international trade commitments.

Challenging Chinese measures affecting electronic payment services (EPS).

- The United States successfully challenged, before a WTO panel, China's restrictions on foreign suppliers of EPS for card-based transactions. EPS enable, facilitate, and manage the flow of information and the transmission of funds between banks that issue credit and debit cards and merchants' banks. Millions of payment card transactions occur every day in China, and, each year, well over $1 trillion worth of electronic payment card transactions are processed in China. China's discriminatory measures severely distort competition and prevent participation by foreign suppliers of EPS for domestic currency payment card transactions. The WTO panel's findings under the General Agreement on Trade in Services make clear that China's pervasive and discriminatory measures deny a level playing field to foreign service providers, including the American EPS providers who are world leaders in this sector.

Ensuring EU compliance with WTO a ruling in support of U.S. high-tech exports to Europe.

- The United States won a significant victory with a WTO panel ruling that the EU had violated its WTO tariff commitments by imposing duties as high as 14 percent on three high-tech products (certain monitors, printers, and set top boxes). The EU took some steps to comply, which have resulted in lower duties on U.S. high-tech exports. The United States has remained vigilant regarding the EU's compliance and will continue to work to ensure that the EU eliminates all duties on the products at issue.

Enhancing access to the EU market for beef.

- The WTO Appellate Body found the EU's ban on U.S. beef to be contrary to its commitments under the WTO Sanitary and Phytosanitary (SPS) Agreement. After the United States subsequently imposed WTO-authorized retaliation, in 2009 the United States and the EU negotiated a Memorandum of Understanding (MOU) that gives U.S. producers of high quality beef substantial duty-free access to the EU market. Phase 2 of the MOU began in August 2012, resulting in an expansion of the tariff-rate quota for high quality beef to more than double its phase 1 size.

Addressing barriers to distilled spirits market access.

- The United States obtained a victory from a WTO panel and the Appellate Body in its challenge to discriminatory Philippine excise taxes on imported distilled spirits. The Philippines taxes imported distilled spirits, such as whiskey and gin, at significantly higher rates than domestic distilled spirits, resulting in a major barrier to market access.

Ensuring a level playing field for the U.S. wind power sector.

- As part of a Section 301 investigation, the United States initiated a WTO case challenging subsidies to China's wind power equipment manufacturers that required the use of local content, at the expense of foreign competitors. The United States held consultations with China in February 2011, and China subsequently terminated the chall-enged subsidy program.

Challenging India's import ban on agricultural products.

- The United States initiated a WTO challenge to India's prohibition on the importation of certain U.S. agricultural products, including poultry meat and chicken eggs. Although India's measure purports to be concerned with preventing avian influenza, the measure does not have a scientific basis and is not in line with international standards. The measure thus appears to be inconsistent with India's obligations under the WTO SPS Agreement.

Challenging Argentina's widespread use of import restrictions.

- The United States initiated a WTO challenge to Argentina's trade restrictive measures, including import licensing requirements apparently adopted for the purpose of trade balancing. These measures adversely affect a broad segment of U.S. industry and billions of dollars in U.S. trade in goods each year to Argentina.

Enforcing the subsidy rules.

- In 2011, the United States submitted information to the WTO on more than 200 subsidy programs in China and 50 subsidy programs in India. China and India are obligated to notify these subsidies on their own but had failed to do so for many years. This was the first time the United States had ever invoked a rarely used provision of the WTO Subsidies Agreement to "counter notify" another WTO member's subsidies to the WTO. These efforts will increase the transparency of the Chinese and Indian subsidy regimes, and will enable U.S. industries and workers to more readily assess the impact of Chinese and Indian subsidies and to make better informed decisions about potential actions to address subsidized imports.

Protection and enforcement of U.S. intellectual property rights (IPR).

- The United States effectively used a wide range of tools in 2011–2012, including the Special 301 Report, the Out of Cycle Notorious Markets Report, bilateral and regional dialogues and fora, joint law enforcement operations, and plurilateral and multilateral agreements and engagement to seek strong protection and enforcement of IPR. These efforts contributed to significant results. For example, the 2012 Special 301 review process examined IPR protection and enforcement in 77 countries, resulting in 40 trading partners being listed in the annual Special 301 Report issued on April 30, 2012. U.S. Government bilateral advocacy before and after the 2011 Special 301 Report encouraged the adoption of significant IPR-related laws or regulations in several countries, such as the enactment in Malaysia of copyright amendments that strengthen copyright protection, as well as increased IPR enforcement, and the promulgation of regulations to protect pharmaceutical test data. In addition, as a result of these efforts, Spain adopted regulations implementing a law to combat piracy over the Internet. Most significant was China's creation of a State Council–level leadership structure, headed by Vice Premier Wang Qishan, to lead and coordinate IPR enforcement across China.

The Out of Cycle Review of Notorious Markets identifies selected markets, including those on the Internet, that reportedly are engaged in piracy and counterfeiting. USTR has identified notorious markets in the Special 301 Report since 2006. In 2010, USTR announced that it would begin publishing the Notorious Market List as an Out of Cycle Review, separately from the annual Special 301 Report. USTR published the first such list in February 2011, as well as a subsequent list in December 2011. Following their inclusion in the February 2011 Notorious Markets List, several markets took action to address the widespread availability of pirated or counterfeit goods, including the Chinese website Baidu (identified in the Notorious Markets List for several years), which entered into a landmark licensing agreement with the United States and other rights holders from the recording industry. At the Ladies Market in Hong Kong, local customs officials took action to remove allegedly infringing goods from the premises, and authorities reported a commitment to continue to undertake enforcement actions at the market. Finally, at the Savelovskiy Market in Russia, management has implemented an action plan to stop the distribution of infringing goods.

The plurilateral Anti-Counterfeiting Trade Agreement, signed in Tokyo on October 1, 2011, will strengthen international cooperation, enforcement practices, and legal frameworks for fighting counterfeiting and piracy when it enters into force. The U.S. trade agreements with Korea and Colombia also include high standards for IPR protection and enforcement. Regional efforts yielded results as well, such as the endorsement by APEC economies of the APEC Effective Practices for Addressing Unauthorized Camcording.

Interagency Trade Enforcement Center.

- In the September 2010 Report to the President on the National Export Initiative, the EPC and TPCC committed to increasing interagency efforts to identify and address unfair foreign trade practices that diminish U.S. exporters' competitiveness in global markets.

For these reasons, in his 2012 State of the Union Address, the President made clear that lasting economic growth requires leveling the playing field for American workers and businesses and called for "the creation of a trade enforcement unit that will be charged with investigating unfair trading practices in countries like China." The President carried out that commitment on February 28, 2012, by signing an Executive Order launching the Interagency Trade Enforcement Center

(ITEC). ITEC brings a "whole-of-government" approach to addressing unfair trade practices and has the following core missions: (1) to serve as the primary forum within the Federal Government for the Office of the U.S. Trade Representative (USTR), Department of Commerce, and other agencies to coordinate the enforcement of U.S. trade rights under international trade agreements and enforcement of domestic trade laws; (2) to coordinate among USTR, Department of Commerce, and other agencies with trade-related responsibilities and the U.S. Intelligence Community the exchange of information related to potential violations of international trade agreements by the United States' foreign trade partners; and (3) to conduct outreach to U.S. workers, businesses and other interested persons to foster greater participation in the identification and reduction or elimination of foreign trade barriers and unfair foreign trade practices.

The ITEC continues to ramp up, and it is expected to be fully operational by the end of 2013. ITEC is designed to help leverage and mobilize resources and expertise across the Federal Government to develop trade enforcement actions that will address unfair foreign trade practices and barriers. The ITEC's interagency personnel constitute an expanded team of language-proficient researchers, subject matter experts, and economic analysts. Most recently, ITEC played a critical role in developing the WTO consultations request regarding China's export subsidies on autos and auto parts (the China Export Bases matter) by providing Chinese-language research, subsidies analysis, and translation support.

Promotion of Stronger, More Sustainable, and More Balanced Growth

In addition to U.S. productivity growth and export competitiveness, the most significant determinant of U.S. export growth over the next few years will be the pace of the United States' main trading partners' economic growth. In the short term, working to sustain a strong global economic recovery will likely deliver the biggest contribution to U.S. export growth.

In the second half of 2011, global growth and trade each slowed sharply as financial stresses in Europe intensified. That weakness carried over to the first half of 2012, but growth is expected to gradually strengthen as financial stresses ease. In 2011, the G-20 focused on the necessary policy adjustments to stimulate a more rapid rebalancing of the global economy. In addition, in November 2011, the G-20 Leaders developed and committed to a policy action plan to stimulate growth and address imbalances. The G-20 is now actively following up on those commitments to ensure that they are fully implemented. At the Leaders' summit in Los Cabos, Mexico, in June 2012, Leaders reviewed progress on implementation and agreed to a new Accountability Assessment Framework to track implementation of past and future commitments. Additionally, Leaders made further commitments aimed at strengthening the recovery and spurring greater demand growth in major trading partners.

Implementation of Key 2011 National Export Strategy Priorities

In addition to maximizing the impact of current Federal Government programs, the June 2011 National Export Strategy highlighted several new priorities on which the TPCC would focus. The TPCC agencies have successfully implemented these initiatives and will continue to deepen their commitment to maximizing their impact in the coming year.

Collaboration with States and Metropolitan Areas

Metropolitan Export Plans (MEPs).

Metropolitan areas produce 84 percent of the nation's exports and are home to unique concentrations of capital, investment, and innovation. According to the Brookings Institution, the 100 largest metropolitan areas alone account for more than 64 percent of the nation's exports, including 75 percent of services exports.[1] Regional economies do not stop at Congressional districts or state boundaries. Moreover, the nature of export data makes it difficult for metropolitan leaders to access a full and accurate picture of an area's industrial export activity, because current export data are based on origin of movement (where goods are shipped from) instead of where goods are produced.

---

1   Emilia Istrate, Jonathan Rothwell, and Bruce Katz, "Export Nation: How U.S. Metros Lead National Export Growth and Boost Competitiveness." (Washington, DC: Brookings Institution, 2010), p. 2.

To localize the NEI and recognize metropolitan centers as the engines driving national export growth, the Department of Commerce has collaborated with the Brookings Institution Metropolitan Policy Program on its effort to help regional civic, business, and political leaders create and implement customized metropolitan export plans (MEPs). These localized export plans apply market intelligence to develop better, targeted, and integrated export-related services and strategies to help regions better connect their firms to global customers, as outlined by their individualized export goals. These MEPs have also outlined the kinds of state and Federal Government reforms needed to support the effective implementation of such plans. Four pilot plans have been completed and made available online: Los Angeles, CA; Portland, OR; Minneapolis, MN; and Syracuse, NY. As a next step, Brookings has developed a metropolitan export strategy template that builds on these pilot MEPs and is working to help facilitate the adoption of export plans in additional markets. Meanwhile, federal agency partners will continue to work with Brookings and metropolitan area leaders to further localize the NEI.

Making Global Local.

Over the past year, U.S. companies have increasingly targeted emerging economies as export destinations in response to the significant downturn in economic growth among industrialized countries. Given its unique role in both foreign assistance and export promotion, USTDA is perfectly positioned to support U.S. businesses interested in entering or expanding their presence in developing and middle-income countries. USTDA's signature IBPP brings foreign delegates on reverse trade missions to the United States, pending upcoming procurements. While in the United States, the delegations observe the design, manufacture, and operation of U.S. products and services that can help them achieve their development goals. Last year alone, USTDA supported 50 reverse trade missions that connected more than 600 foreign delegates with more than 1,000 U.S. company representatives across the country.

To increase awareness of USTDA's export-promoting programs, USTDA launched Making Global Local, an initiative designed to connect towns and cities across the country with USTDA. By building strategic partnerships, USTDA and local business organizations can support the creation of high-paying jobs through the growth of U.S. exports. Partner organizations include local non-profit or governmental entities that have demonstrated a commitment to supporting the creation of jobs in their community through the growth of U.S. exports, such as World Trade Centers, local non-profit economic development organizations, state or municipal governmental entities, and others. USTDA currently has 17 partner organizations located in California, Colorado, Georgia, Louisiana, Maryland, Mississippi, Missouri, New York, Pennsylvania, Vermont, Virginia, and Washington. By understanding USTDA's programs, these partner organizations can help companies in their communities maximize the benefits of working with USTDA.

New State and local members of the President's Export Council.

The President increased the membership of the President's Export Council, his chief advisory council on exporting, to include representation of the National Governors Association and the United States Conference of Mayors.

Export.gov Next Generation

Export.gov is the Federal Government's export assistance portal bringing together export promotion resources across agencies. Pursuant to the President's "No Wrong Door Directive" policy mentioned earlier, the Export.gov and BusinessUSA. gov teams are working together to develop a set of common standards to be applied to federal content that will make it easier for businesses to find and tap federal programs and resources. An early version of BusinessUSA.gov is already helping businesses. The next generation of Export.gov will be released in January 2013 as part of the BusinessUSA.gov family. This technology will be used in the next version of BusinessUSA.gov.

Congressional Approval of Korea, Colombia, and Panama Trade Agreements

In 2011, the Administration secured Congressional approval of market-opening trade agreements with Korea, Colombia, and Panama. This achievement resulted from the Administration's concerted efforts during the previous two years to take steps that made the agreements better serve American workers and businesses and better reflect American values. The United States–Korea Free Trade Agreement entered into force on March 15, 2012. The United States–Colombia Trade Promotion Agreement entered into force on May 15, 2012. The United States–Panama Trade Promotion Agreement entered into force on October 31, 2012. The TPCC agencies have planned increased outreach to SMEs to raise awareness of important new opportunities in those markets.

Improvement of the U.S. Supply Chain Infrastructure

As noted in the 2011 NES Report, America's highways, railways, bridges, waterways, runways, and ports are at the beginning of a very long global logistics chain. Improving and maintaining a globally competitive, user-focused U.S. supply chain infrastructure that is reliable, resilient, and able to offer the necessary capacity is critical to the success of the NEI. The following are some of the actions that have taken place since the 2011 NES Report that promise significant improvements to the U.S. supply chain infrastructure.

Passage of surface and aviation transportation reauthorization legislation.

The 2011 NES Report contained a TPCC recommendation that surface and aviation transportation reauthorization legislation be passed. This recommendation has been achieved, and the two acts are briefly described below. Together, they address the accumulated U.S. infrastructure deficit hampering exports. They also provide opportunities for investments supporting all the modes of transportation that affect U.S. competitiveness in international trade and address the requirements of ports, intermodal yards, and "last mile" connections in which export cargos are handed off from one mode to another. Finally, they focus infrastructure investments on the parts of the system that can have the greatest payoff in enhancing U.S. economic competitiveness.

On July 6, 2012, President Obama signed the Moving Ahead for Progress in the 21st Century Act (MAP-21), authorizing $105 billion for surface transportation investment. A major focus of MAP-21 is improving freight transportation; it also introduces a new emphasis on performance management. The centerpiece of MAP-21 is the $44 billion National Highway Performance Program, which requires States to set performance targets for maintaining and improving the National Highway System—the central core of the Nation's highway network most heavily used by freight shippers. MAP-21 also directs the U.S. Department of Transportation to establish a National Freight Strategic Plan, including a National Freight Conditions and Performance Report that will help guide transportation infrastructure investments to the projects that will have the most beneficial effects on freight transportation. MAP-21 authorizes $1.75 billion for the Department of Transportation's infrastructure loan program, which is expected to support $17 billion in loans and to leverage an additional $20 to $30 billion in infrastructure investment. MAP-21 also authorizes $500 million for the Projects of National and Regional Significance grant program, which can be used for highway, freight rail, and certain kinds of port projects.

On February 14, 2012, the President signed the Federal Aviation Administration (FAA) Modernization and Reform Act of 2012, authorizing $63 billion for the Nation's aviation system over four years. The FAA bill will provide the stability and predictability to ensure that critical aviation safety programs, NextGen (the FAA program for transitioning air traffic control and navigation to state-of-the-art satellite technology), and aviation infrastructure investments move forward. Although the FAA bill does not provide funding specifically for NextGen, the FAA bill does include NextGen within facilities and equipment funding. (The President's 2013 Budget contains nearly $1 billion for NextGen.)

Expanded export container availability.

The 2011 NES Report contained a TPCC recommendation to expand export container availability. The report noted that it was often costly for exporters to gain access to the containers they need to meet the worldwide demand for their products and that many exporters are farmers and manufacturers located in rural areas.

- The U.S. Department of Transportation (DOT) has helped to address this issue by providing credit assistance through its Private Activity Bond program for inland port facilities in the Midwest. DOT has provided $1.6 billion in Private Activity Bond authority for two inland ports in Joliet, IL, and Kansas City, MO. These inland ports allow double-stack container trains to move marine containers directly from West Coast ports to Midwest inland ports, where the containers are unloaded into trucks for final delivery. The inland ports then have a ready supply of empty containers that can be filled with grain and manufactured goods for export.

- In December 2010, the Federal Maritime Commission (FMC) completed a fact-finding investigation of vessel capacity and container availability issues, identifying a number of FMC resources that shippers and carriers can voluntarily use to resolve availability problems.

- The FMC also approved a recommendation from the cabinet-level Committee on the Marine Transportation System (CMTS) to form a container availability working group that will collaborate with all parts of the intermodal industry to develop additional solutions to these issues for U.S. exporters. The CMTS is developing an interagency process to monitor the general availability of containers in the United States, and, if necessary, will develop recommended actions for the TPCC and other interested parties to prevent or ameliorate ocean container shortages. On behalf of the CMTS, the FMC is leading this interagency effort.

- To provide U.S. agricultural exporters with data on the availability of containers, the Department of Agriculture's Agricultural Marketing Service has begun publishing a weekly Ocean Shipping Container Availability Report that provides data on the availability of ocean containers at 18 intermodal locations around the United States, including inland points such as Minneapolis, MN; Kansas City, MO; and Chicago, IL. Data provided in the report indicate that the worldwide supply of containers grew by 7.0 percent in 2010 and by 8.5 percent in 2011.

Department of Commerce Advisory Committee on Supply Chain Competitiveness.

The Department of Commerce has established, in close cooperation with DOT, the Advisory Committee on Supply Chain Competitiveness and has appointed members. The Committee will advise on the development and administration of programs and policies to increase the competitiveness of U.S. supply chains, including programs and policies to expand U.S. exports of goods, services, and technology related to supply chains to support U.S. export growth and competitiveness and improve U.S. supply chain competitiveness in the domestic and global economy. The Advisory Committee on Supply Chain Competitiveness held its inaugural meeting on October 19, 2012.

Investing in transportation infrastructure.

The U.S. Department of Transportation is making it easier for American companies to export goods and services to consumers around the globe through its Transportation Investments Generating Economic Recovery (TIGER) competitive infrastructure grant program. Through four rounds of TIGER grants beginning in 2010, the Administration has invested $953 million in U.S. freight transportation infrastructure. TIGER grant awards have gone to 50 freight-related projects on significant freight corridors, including rail, port, and highway projects. More than a third of that funding—$354 million—went to 25 U.S. port projects from coast to coast. These freight-related projects will help speed delivery of products from American factories, farms, and businesses to customers across the United States and around the world.

Increased Administration Focus on Travel and Tourism's Potential

Travel and tourism is one of the bright spots of the U.S. economy. In 2011, travel and tourism accounted for 7.5 million jobs in the United States. Of this, an estimated 1.2 million jobs were supported by international travelers, who spent a record $153 billion, producing a $43 billion surplus in U.S. trade in travel services. In 2011, U.S. travel and tourism receipts (i.e., exports) accounted for 25 percent of all U.S. services exports.

President Obama signed an executive order in January 2012 creating a Task Force on Travel and Competitiveness that was charged with developing a National Travel and Tourism Strategy for the United States. This Task Force, jointly chaired by the Secretaries of Commerce and Interior, and comprised of twelve agencies of the Federal Government, developed a whole-of-government approach to maximize the potential of travel and tourism to grow the economy, generate exports, and create jobs. The National Travel and Tourism Strategy was released in April 2012 and is being implemented by the relevant federal agencies and coordinated through the Tourism Policy Council, which is chaired by the Secretary of Commerce.

The National Travel and Tourism Strategy is already producing results. U.S. travel exports continue to outpace other U.S. exports of goods and services. Through the first eight months of 2012, travel exports increased a solid 8.3 percent compared to 2011. This growth was supported by action across the Federal Government. Notable accomplishments are delineated below.

- The Department of State has reduced visa wait times in key markets. In China, interview wait times have been reduced to an average of five days, despite a 37 percent increase in visa demand. In addition, wait times in Brazil have been brought down by 98 percent, from a high of 140 days in São Paulo, to just two days in September 2012, despite a 37 percent increase in year-on-year demand. Worldwide, 88 percent of visa applicants are interviewed within three weeks of submitting their applications.

- Taiwan was admitted into the Visa Waiver Program, which will make it easier for its citizens to travel to the United States and drive demand for travel.

- The Departments of Commerce, Treasury, State, and Homeland Security supported and coordinated with the Corporation for Travel Promotion, doing business as Brand USA as the new corporation began its international promotion efforts in Canada, Japan, and the United Kingdom. Support included disbursing federal matching funds to Brand USA, as authorized by the Travel Promotion Act of 2009, as amended.

- Over 325,000 new members have access to the U.S. Customs and Border Protection (CBP) Trusted Traveler Programs. The Department of Homeland Security processed 500,000 more Global Entry passengers in 2012, compared to the same time period in 2011. South Korea joined the Global Entry program on June 12, 2012. Global Entry is now available at 40 airports.

- As of the end of November 2012, over 4 million passengers received Transportation Security Administration (TSA) PreCheck™ expedited screening at 32 participating domestic airports in partnership with participating U.S. air carriers and CBP. By the end of 2012, TSA expects to bring TSA PreCheck™ to a total of 35 domestic airports. Certain frequent travelers from Alaska Airlines, American Airlines, Delta Air Lines, United Airlines, US Airways and certain members of CBP's Trusted Traveler programs, including Global Entry, SENTRI, and NEXUS who are U.S. citizens are eligible to participate. In addition, Canadian citizens traveling domestically in the U.S. who are members of NEXUS are qualified to participate as well.

- The U.S. Commercial Service assisted nearly 500 U.S. travel suppliers in meeting with over 2,500 foreign tour operators, travel agents, and media. Over 70 exporters signed 250 contracts with overseas tour operators in the first half of 2012.

- The Department of State incorporated travel and tourism as part of its public diplomacy efforts, with embassies around the world communicating that the United States wants and welcomes international visitors. The Department of State's "Fifty States in Fifty Days" initiative showcased travel opportunities throughout the United States, and is being followed by other initiatives with themes attractive to potential visitors.

- In October 2012, the Department of State hosted a conference on travel and tourism, as part of its Global Business series. This strategy dialogue brought together representatives of the Departments of Commerce, Homeland Security, and State with a broad spectrum of private sector stakeholders to discuss the National Strategy on Travel and Tourism and other policy and program improvements to facilitate growth in travel and tourism exports. At the conference, Secretary Clinton and Secretary Napolitano announced the inclusion of Taiwan in the Visa Waiver Program.

- The Department of Commerce provided data critical to measuring progress of the Strategy, including international arrivals to the United States and estimates of the total impact of travel and tourism on the economy, and job creation. In addition, the Department developed Dashboard of Travel indicators to measure performance of key government services and programs supporting international travel to the United States, which is available to the public on the Department's website.

Chapter 2:
The EPC's Plan for Maximizing the Effectiveness of Federal Programs

Economic Snapshot: U.S. Small Businesses Power More of America's Exports.

The National Export Initiative (NEI) places a special emphasis on helping small businesses overcome the hurdles to entering new markets.[2] Because small businesses are responsible for generating 64 percent of all net new private sector jobs,[3] those businesses serve as the engine for the U.S. economy, and enhancing their export participation will help ensure that the nation's economic recovery stays on track. In the March 2010 Executive Order establishing the NEI, the President directed the Export Promotion Cabinet, as its first priority, to develop programs "designed to enhance export assistance to SMEs, including programs that improve information and other technical assistance to first-time exporters."

A record 287,000 U.S. small- and medium-sized enterprises (SME) exported in 2010 (98 percent of all exporters), a total increase of more than 16,600 SMEs over 2009.[4] Moreover, SMEs continue to grow their share of overall U.S. exports, composing 34 percent of total export value in 2010, up from 27 percent in 2002 (see figure 3).

Early estimates indicate that this trend continued into 2011, with the SME share of exports increasing further.

This trend is affected by the prominent role SMEs play in competitive industries, such as environmental technologies and medical equipment. Additionally, the growth of the Internet economy has allowed SMEs to better market their products and services internationally at a fraction of the previous cost.

The trend shows that America's SMEs have what it takes to compete successfully in the global economy. The latest available Census data show that the value of exports by U.S. SMEs in 2010 was more than $380 billion, an increase of more than 24 percent from 2009. Additionally, the number of identified SME exporters increased by 6 percent in 2010 to 287,000 firms.[5]

Entering the export game can be daunting, however, especially for SMEs. It is telling that of the 287,000 U.S. SMEs that export, more than 58.5 percent export to only one market, usually to Canada or Mexico. Many of the most promising export opportunities are in more distant emerging economies that are growing more than twice as fast as advanced economies, thereby increasing emerging economies' ability to purchase U.S. goods and services. Free trade agreement (FTA) partners in Central America and South America, for example, can be especially attractive markets to which U.S. SMEs may begin or expand their export sales because of the reduction and elimination of trade barriers and speedier customs procedures under U.S. FTAs. The Trade Promotion Coordinating Committee (TPCC) agencies have launched a free online FTA tariff tool

---

2   See Exec. Order No. 13534, Section 3(a).

3   Small Business Administration, Office of Advocacy, Frequently Asked Questions, September 2012, http://www.sba.gov/advocacy/7495/29581

4   U.S. Department of Commerce, U.S. Census Bureau, "A Profile of U.S. Importing and Exporting Companies, 2009-2010," April 12, 2012, p. 11-13 (Exhibits 1a and 1b, 2010 Exports by Company Type and Employment Type)

5   U.S. Department of Commerce, U.S. Census Bureau, "A Profile of U.S. Importing and Exporting Companies, 2009-2010," April 12, 2012, p. 11-13 (Exhibits 1a and 1b, 2010 Exports by Company Type and Employment Type)

to help SMEs plan for entry into FTA partner markets (Export.gov/FTA/ftatarifftool/index.asp). In both emerging markets and FTA partner countries, the U.S. Government can help companies, particularly smaller firms, find prospective foreign buyers or business partners and can provide financing solutions that help companies manage the risks of exporting.

Given a challenging global economy, the United States must re-double efforts to expand its national base of SME exporters to sustain this historic progress. Relative to large firms, growth in the value of SME exports is more dependent on the growth of the net number of new exporters.[6] Additionally, SME exporters outperform their non-exporting SME counterparts in several measures including higher revenues, faster revenue growth, and higher labor productivity.

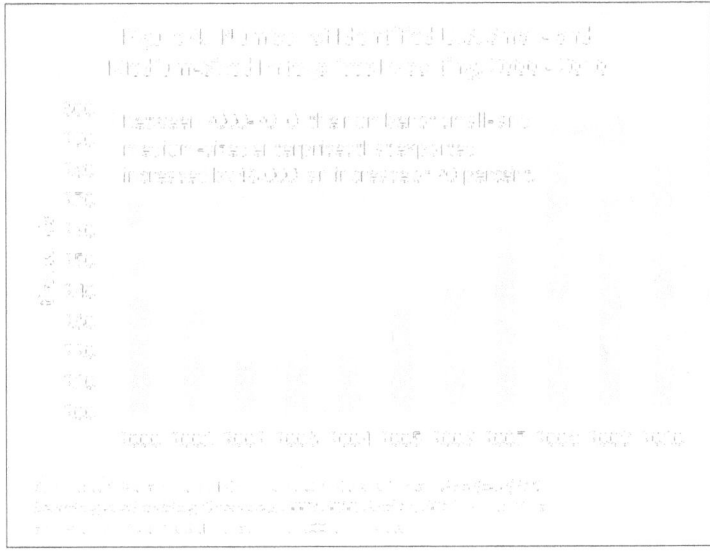

SMEs often struggle with real and perceived challenges to exporting. Just over one percent or 287,000 of the approximately 27.9 million small businesses in the United States[7] currently export. Although the number of SME exporters in the United States has been steadily increasing over the past decade (up 20 percent since 2000, see figure 4), exporting is not as much a part the national business culture for U.S. SMEs as it is for their competitors in many other markets. The large, easily accessible U.S. domestic market contributes to this. In fact, in an investigation on SME exporters in 2010, the U.S. International Trade Commission (ITC) found that SMEs in the European Union play a larger role in manufactured exports relative to U.S. SMEs for almost all manufacturing industries.[8]

Many SMEs think exporting is too burdensome or too risky, or they just do not know where to start. SMEs are more likely to need external financing to undertake an export transaction. SMEs can also find it more difficult to get information about foreign markets and face higher risks from foreign trade barriers and unfair trade practices in contrast with larger firms' access to market intelligence and their direct presence in foreign markets. Many U.S. SMEs could benefit from learning more about international market opportunities and relevant federal resources.

Export Promotion Cabinet (EPC) Priorities for Maximizing the Effectiveness of Federal Programs

In a February 2012 Memorandum to federal agencies, the President directed the EPC to develop strategies to maximize the effectiveness of federal programs supporting trade and investment under the NEI.[9] In July 2012, the EPC finalized its plan for maximizing the effectiveness of federal programs that support trade and investment. This plan was the product of an unprecedented collaboration among agencies that comprise the EPC and the TPCC.[10]

---

6   International Trade Commission, Small and Medium-Sized Enterprises: Overview of Participation in U.S. Exports, January 2010, p. i, http://www.usitc.gov/publications/332/pub4125.pdf.

7   Small Business Administration, Office of Advocacy, Frequently Asked Questions, September 2012, http://www.sba.gov/advocacy/7495/29581.

8   International Trade Commission, Small and Medium-Sized Enterprises: U.S. and EU Export Activities, and Barriers and Opportunities Experienced by U.S. Firms, July 2010, p. 2-14, http://www.usitc.gov/publications/332/pub4169.pdf.

9   http://www.whitehouse.gov/the-press-office/2012/02/17/presidential-memorandum-maximizing-effectiveness-federal-programs-and-fu.

10 The EPC consists of the heads of the following 17 agencies: the Departments of State, the Treasury, Agriculture, Commerce, Labor, Energy, Homeland Security, and Transportation; Office of Management and Budget; Office of the U.S. Trade Representative; National Economic Council; National Security Council; Council of Economic Advisors; Export-Import Bank of the United States; Small Business Administration; Overseas Private Investment Corporation; and the U.S. Trade and Development Agency. The TPCC consists of all of the Export Promotion Cabinet agencies plus four additional agencies: the Department of Defense, the Department of the Interior, the Agency for International Development, and the Environmental Protection Agency.

The EPC action plan outlines the framework for a more robust commitment to facilitating the success of U.S. SME exporters. Through this action plan, the EPC and TPCC will increase the effectiveness of federal export assistance by launching new efforts aimed at SME exporters, by expanding the reach and impact of domestic trade counseling, and by providing new and more strategic approaches to delivering export services. When the action plan is fully executed over the next few years, the Federal Government will be better positioned to support the growth and competitiveness of SME exporters in global markets.

Goal 1: Increase the National Base of Small Business Exporters

The EPC set the goal of increasing the national base of SME exporters by 50,000 firms by 2017.[11] The EPC action plan outlines three key objectives of a collaborative interagency approach to impact the entry, success, and growth of SME exporters. As identified through a series of ITC reports in 2010, these elements reflect the top three barriers for SME exporters: (1) problems identifying foreign business opportunities and federal export assistance resources, (2) shortage of capital to finance exports, and (3) limited information on how to analyze markets and contact potential foreign customers.

Objective #1: Develop a national marketing campaign targeting SME exporters.

The EPC/TPCC agencies will generate a national marketing campaign to educate SME businesses on the benefits of exporting and the availability of federal export assistance resources. This message will be disseminated in novel ways, including through distributing marketing materials, leveraging the 2012 Economic Census, providing private sector and trade association partners with outreach guides and marketing materials, and launching a major social media outreach campaign.

Objective #2: Expand access to small business trade financing.

The difficulties that SMEs face in attempting to access trade financing can be traced to two overarching causes: the lack of profitability for larger lenders and the perception that trade financing is too complex for smaller lenders. The Export-Import Bank of the United States, the Small Business Administration, the Foreign Agricultural Service/U.S. Department of Agriculture, and Overseas Private Investment Corporation will launch a "Global Business Solutions" program that will develop unified U.S. Government domestic, export, and investment financing solution packages that will better meet the needs of SMEs and lenders alike. Organized in a problem-solution format that can be quickly understood, rather than sorted by U.S. agency, the packages will facilitate the ability of commercial lenders to profitably meet the financing needs of SME exporters. Additionally, the EPC/TPCC agencies will work with banking regulators to provide in-depth training to community banks in order to expand the financial infrastructure offering trade-related products throughout the country.

Objective #3: Enhance trade promotion support for SME exporters.

To increase the number of SME exporters taking advantage of federal export promotion services, EPC/TPCC agencies will develop a U.S. trade show brand to attract more foreign buyers and U.S. companies to domestic and overseas trade shows; encourage and support SMEs to exploit opportunities offered at U.S. trade shows; and facilitate the development of a virtual marketplace and virtual trade missions to make it easier and less expensive for SMEs to reach foreign partners and buyers.

---

11 In 2010, the number of SME exporters stood at about 287,000. One can expect that cumulative nominal export growth will yield an increase in the number of SME exporters of roughly 17 percent over 2010 levels, corresponding to an additional 50,000 SME exporters by 2017. In the span of a decade (from 2000 to 2010), the United States saw roughly 48,000 new SME exporters enter the market, so this growth would support the same number of SME exporters in half the time (5 years instead of 10 years).

Goal 2: Make It Easier for U.S. Businesses to Access Federal Export Assistance

The EPC action plan outlines four objectives that, when executed, will align and optimize federal domestic field offices with the goal of making it easier for U.S. businesses to access federal export assistance. The goal is to improve the way the Federal Government interacts with its customers through the expansion of the availability of export counseling through a nationwide network of integrated physical and virtual providers.

Objective #4: Expand the reach of federal export assistance and facilitate more efficient delivery of services.

The EPC/TPCC agencies will ensure the full use of the approximately 1,500 federal agency domestic field offices and resource partners' business development and export assistance offices, including the addition of hundreds of federal business development offices that do not currently, in a systematic fashion, provide export-related counseling and services. The EPC/TPCC agencies will establish a national protocol for client services that will optimize how clients are served across federal domestic field offices and increase the level of coordination among these offices by including a clear process for referring clients to the correct federal services.

Objective #5: Institute a national training program for federal trade counselors and resource partners.

The EPC/TPCC agencies will execute a nationwide training program for federal personnel and resource partners that will (1) help domestic field offices understand the importance of exporting for SMEs and the range of federal export assistance available to their clients and (2) provide relevant domestic offices with the capacity to offer various levels of direct export counseling, services, and other assistance.

Objective #6: Develop and integrate a virtual "one-stop shop" for federal export assistance.

The EPC/TPCC agencies will commit to fully developing BusinessUSA.gov into a virtual one-stop shop for federal export assistance that will integrate the content of Export.gov, as well as the operational content of relevant agencies' websites. This shared Web platform will make it easier for U.S. businesses to (1) receive a personalized experience in order to help them access the most relevant products and services offered by federal agencies, (2) provide targeted lead generation to U.S. exporters through U.S. federal domestic field offices, (3) create an interagency data-sharing environment, and (4) improve how federal agencies and their business counseling resource partners interact with U.S. business clients.

Objective #7: Develop pilot performance measures to track progress.

The EPC/TPCC agencies will establish pilot methodologies to measure the level of collaboration and customer service satisfaction in domestic field operations across regional networks.

Goal 3: Improve Strategic Delivery of Federal Export Assistance

To overcome hurdles related to the strategic allocation of overseas resources, the EPC action plan includes a framework for launching biannual interagency strategic discussions on resource allocations in U.S. embassies and consulates. The goal is to improve the way the Federal Government makes major resource decisions, delivers export promotion services overseas, and partners with the private sector in priority export markets.

Objective #8: Increase interagency coordination and strategic alignment on the allocation of overseas resources.

The EPC/TPCC agencies will foster increased interagency coordination and cooperation around the strategic allocation of federal resources in foreign markets, including the proactive identification of existing or emerging priority markets for the provision of enhanced economic, commercial, agricultural, and trade services. The EPC/TPCC agencies will track progress on both reallocation of resources and the development of best practices that will improve the level of interagency coordination and collaboration with the private sector.

Objective# 9: Develop and pilot new paradigms for delivering economic, commercial, agricultural, and trade services.

The EPC/TPCC agencies will pilot new paradigms for providing export assistance, both domestically and overseas, with a significant focus on developing new ways to collaborate with private sector and non-profit partners. Sister City Export Partnerships will help to drive U.S. exporter interest to smaller but growing markets by connecting these markets' diaspora communities with tailored programs from domestic federal trade offices. Through a Community Partnerships Program, Department of Commerce domestic trade counselors and Foreign Service Officers will be embedded within domestic non-profit entities such as chambers of commerce and economic development organizations to better coordinate federal export assistance with local businesses.

Chapter 3:
Looking Over the Horizon in a Rapidly Changing Global Marketplace

Economic Snapshot: Robust Emerging Market Growth and Strong Foreign Competition Define a Global Marketplace Full of Both Opportunities and Challenges

Global Market Trends

Moving into the third year of the National Export Initiative (NEI), slower economic growth in foreign markets is likely to affect the nation's ability to export. The International Monetary Fund (IMF) predicts that world gross domestic product (GDP) growth will slow to 3.5 percent in 2012, declining from 3.9 percent in 2011.[12] The European Union, which accounts for about 22 percent of U.S. exports of goods and services, for example, could experience zero economic growth in 2012, with a contraction of 0.3 percent forecast for the Euro Area. Also, the IMF projects that 16 of the top 20 U.S. merchandise export markets have slower GDP growth in 2012 than in 2011. These 16 markets represent more than 64 percent of U.S. total merchandise exports.

Nevertheless, economic growth in emerging and developing markets remains near 6 percent, pointing to several resilient and growing markets that U.S. exporters should be targeting in the near and medium term. More than 95 percent of the world's population and 80 percent of global demand[13] is now outside of the United States. Nominal world imports of goods and services, excluding U.S. imports, increased 200 percent from 2001 to 2011.[14] Forecast 2013 growth ranges from 7.2 percent in developing Asia, to 5.7 percent in Sub-Saharan Africa, 3.6 percent in the Middle East and North Africa, and 3.9 percent in Latin America and the Caribbean.[15] The 21 members[16] of APEC, for example, account for 54 percent of the world's total GDP and 44 percent of the world's trade. Nine of the top 15 U.S. export markets for goods are APEC Member Economies and APEC members account for about 60 percent of overall U.S. exports.[17]

A major factor driving emerging market growth is the emergence of new middle-class consumers. The global middle class is expected to grow from 1.8 billion in 2009 to 3.2 billion by 2020, which should sustain global consumption and import demand.[18] At the same time, emerging markets are improving their business environments.

Foreign Competition

In addition to global market and industry trends, an accurate assessment of the challenges that both large and small U.S. exporters face must include an understanding of the resources and support that foreign governments provide to their exporting companies. Mature industrial competitors continue to view exports as a top priority and are continually focusing and improving their programs. At the same time, other industrialized countries (e.g., Korea) and some of the new large growth markets (e.g., China and India) have entered the arena in major ways.

---

12 International Monetary Fund, World Economic Outlook database, October 2012, Table 1.1, "Overview of the World Economic Outlook Projections," p. 2.
13 International Monetary Fund, World Economic Outlook database.
14 United Nations Conference on Trade and Development (UNCTAD), UNCTADstat, "Values and Shares of Merchandise Exports and Imports, Annual, 1948–2011," found online at http://unctadstat.unctad.org/TableViewer/tableView.aspx?ReportId=101; United Nations Conference on Trade and Development (UNCTAD), UNCTADstat, "Values, Shares and Growth of Exports and Imports of Total Services, Annual, 1980–2011," found online at http://unctadstat.unctad.org/TableViewer/tableView.aspx?ReportId=17648.
15 International Monetary Fund, World Economic Outlook database, July 2012, Table 1, "Overview of the World Economic Outlook Projections," p. 2.
16 Note: APEC's 21 Member Economies are Australia; Brunei Darussalam; Canada; Chile; China; Hong Kong, China; Indonesia; Japan; Republic of Korea; Malaysia; Mexico; New Zealand; Papua New Guinea; Peru; The Republic of the Philippines; The Russian Federation; Singapore; Chinese Taipei; Thailand; the United States of America; and Viet Nam
17 Office of the U.S. Trade Representative, "U.S.-APEC Trade Facts," http://www.ustr.gov/countries-regions/japan-korea-apec/apec/us-apec-trade-facts
18 Mario Pezzini, "An Emerging Middle Class," OECD Observer, 2012. http://www.oecdobserver.org/news/fullstory.php/aid/3681/An_emerging_middle_class.html.

Export financing

The June 2012 Export-Import Bank of the United States (Ex-Im Bank) annual competitiveness report[19] indicates that, although Ex-Im Bank has remained competitive with record-breaking authorizations in support of U.S. exports and jobs, significant challenges are emerging in the form of vastly increasing volumes of export financing coming from competitor countries' export credit agencies.

Members of Ex-Im Bank's 2012 Advisory Committee identified these challenges, and the U.S. private sector's concerns, in the statement that they submitted to Congress on the findings of the 2012 competitiveness report, as follows:

> "Equally as important are Benchmarking Study findings confirming the observations in last year's Report on the existence and rapid growth of unregulated sectors of government export credit. Regulated OECD country activity, at $94 billion, now constitutes just over a third of global government export credit. Non-regulated OECD activity (untied, market window and investment financing) now affords an additional $92 billion annually, and lending from non-OECD players such as China, India and Brazil is at least $64 billion and perhaps much more. The Advisory Committee shares the Report's concern about the size and clear challenge of these burgeoning new export credit areas, which may impact the ability of U.S. exporters to fully compete in this rapidly evolving and non-transparent framework. We fully agree that the second year of the Benchmarking Study be completed with a focus on further understanding these alternative financing vehicles and advancing greater transparency on the part of all of the relevant ECAs."

In an effort to ensure a level playing field in the provision of officially supported export credits, and to ensure that U.S. workers and companies do not lose sales because of unfair foreign government financing, the Treasury Department has been leading the Administration's efforts to implement the export credit commitment made in the May 2012 U.S.–China Strategic and Economic Dialogue (S&ED). At the S&ED, the United States and China agreed to "establish an international working group of major providers of export financing to make concrete progress towards a set of international guidelines on the provision of official export financing, with the goal of concluding an agreement by 2014."[20]

Manufacturing and services sector export promotion

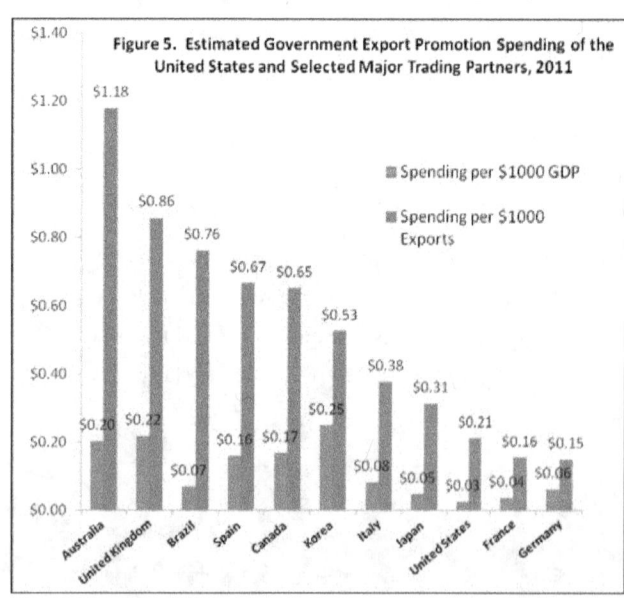

Figure 5. Estimated Government Export Promotion Spending of the United States and Selected Major Trading Partners, 2011

In the spring of 2012, the Department of Commerce's International Trade Administration (ITA) conducted an analysis of competitiveness impacts of foreign government trade promotion programs comparable to ITA export promotion services. This ITA study reviewed the export promotion practices of 11 countries from a wide range of geographic regions and developmental categories, including: mature industrialized countries (e.g., Japan and European countries), newly industrialized countries (e.g., Korea), and large growth markets (e.g., China and Brazil).

Figure 5 compares spending on export promotion relative to both the size of each economy and each country's overall national exports of goods and services. The blue bars represent each country's government-related export promotion spending per $1,000 of GDP. This comparison shows that the United States spends the least at $0.03 per $1,000 of GDP. Korea ($0.25) and

---

19 June 2011 Report to the U.S. Congress on Export Credit Competition and the Export-Import Bank of the United States for the period January 1, 2010, through December 31, 2010. http://www.exim.gov/about/reports/compet/documents/2010_Competitiveness_Report.pdf.

20 U.S. Department of the Treasury, Fourth Meeting of the U.S.–China Strategic and Economic Dialogue, Joint U.S.-China Economic Track Fact Sheet, June 4, 2012, http://www.treasury.gov/press-center/press-releases/Pages/tg1567.aspx

the United Kingdom ($0.22) spend the most per $1,000 of GDP. The red bars represent each country's export promotion spending per $1,000 of overall national exports of goods and services. In this comparison, the United States ranks third to last at $0.21 per $1,000 of exports. France and Germany are the only other countries in the study that spend less on export promotion per $1,000 of exports.

This ITA analysis indicates that U.S. Government expenditures on export promotion are small relative to other countries' expenditures when the size of the economy and the value of exports are taken into account.

Staying Ahead of the Curve: U.S. Government Strategies

Given these changes in markets and in foreign competition, the U.S. Government must employ focused and nimble strategies and tactics for keeping markets open, concentrating its efforts in priority markets and sectors and competing for job-creating inward investment. As noted in Chapter 2, as a result of the Export Promotion Cabinet's (EPC) action plan, Trade Promotion Coordinating Committee (TPCC) agencies are working to expand awareness of growth markets and to create more opportunities for U.S. companies to meet foreign buyers. Simultaneously, and consistent with U.S. obligations under international agreements, they are also expanding financing that helps companies manage the risks of exporting. In addition, the new ITEC provides additional resources to ensure that all of our trading partners play by WTO rules and abide by their obligations, including commitments to maintain open markets on a non-discriminatory basis, and to follow rules-based procedures in a transparent way. (see pp. 11–12).

Improve the Targeting of Infrastructure Projects

ITA and the State Department's Commercial and Business Affairs Office have launched an effort to more effectively identify, target, promote, and help U.S. companies secure prime contracts and subcontracts. The goal is to utilize the tools available to the Federal Government working in concert with foreign governments and the private sector (domestically and abroad) to improve U.S. companies' ability to secure infrastructure contracts overseas. A core group of agencies (The Departments of Commerce, State, Energy, and Transportation; U.S. Trade and Development Agency (USTDA); Ex-Im Bank; Overseas Private Investment Corporation (OPIC); and Small Business Administration (SBA)) is looking at ways the U.S. Government can develop a whole-of-government action plan to help U.S. companies know about and bid on contracts or subcontracts for key infrastructure projects. If successful, the pilot may be expanded to more countries and projects, as well as to longer-term bilateral relationship building activities. In September 2012, the Department of State hosted a global infrastructure conference where TPCC agencies brought together foreign project sponsors and U.S. companies to raise awareness about opportunities in this sector. The TPCC agencies will continue to convene such conferences and periodic outreach in the coming year.

Strengthen Asia-Pacific Policy and Promotion Efforts

Rapid economic development in Asia is a major factor behind the Administration's increasing focus on the Asia-Pacific region. Indicative of the region's growing importance to the United States, major policy initiatives to expand trade, remove trade and investment barriers, and strengthen commercial ties in the region are discussed throughout this report. For example, as noted, the entry into force of the United States–Korea Free Trade Agreement (KORUS) in March 2012 is expected to increase annual U.S. exports to Korea by up to $11 billion (see p. 36). The United States is now leading and seeking to conclude the negotiation of the Trans-Pacific Partnership Agreement, which promises to be one of the most ambitious and state-of-the art trade agreements globally (see p. 6 and p. 50). The United States leveraged its leadership as the host of APEC in 2011, achieving many concrete results (see p. 6–7 and pp. 50, 51). To further demonstrate the United States' commitment to deepen its economic engagement with Southeast Asia, the President again attended the East Asia

Summit and co-chaired the U.S.-Association of Southeast Asian Nations (ASEAN) Leaders Meeting in Cambodia (see p. 36) and visited other ASEAN countries. At this year's U.S.-ASEAN Leaders Meeting, President Obama and the ten ASEAN Leaders launched the U.S.-ASEAN Expanded Economic Engagement (E3) initiative, a new framework for economic cooperation designed to expand trade and investment ties, create new business opportunities and jobs in all eleven countries, and facilitate ASEAN readiness to undertake high standard trade agreements. And the United States has continued to prioritize its engagement with China on key trade policy and investment issues through the U.S.-China Joint Commission on Commerce and Trade (JCCT) (see p. 52) and the U.S.-China Strategic & Economic Dialogue (see p. 52).

Given the Administration's commitment to strengthened economic engagement in the region, TPCC agencies are repositioning significant resources to the Asia-Pacific. In 2011, the Department of Commerce's U.S. & Foreign Commercial Service (U.S. Commercial Service) undertook a review of its worldwide presence. Upon receiving Congressional approval, the U.S. Commercial Service began implementing its plan to reposition resources to NEI priority markets in early FY 2012. This has resulted in a significant shift of resources to posts in the Asia-Pacific region, with particular emphasis on the China and ASEAN markets. The U.S. Commercial Service in China is by far the Commerce Department's most heavily staffed post in the world.

Informal dialogues are also critical to strengthening U.S. trading relationships in the region. In November 2011, ITA launched the U.S.-Indonesia Commercial Dialogue with the Indonesian Coordinating Ministry for Economic Affairs, with meetings including issues such as the ease of doing business in Indonesia and developing a capacity-building work stream on renewable energy. ITA also has had success with a business ethics program in the APEC SME Working Group which it plans to expand to all ASEAN countries during the Indonesia host year of APEC in 2013 through the Philippines host year of APEC in 2015.

Strengthen Africa Commercial Engagement

In June 2012, President Obama announced the U.S. Strategy Toward Sub-Saharan Africa, which includes four pillars: (1) strengthening democratic institutions; (2) spurring economic growth, trade, and investment; (3) advancing peace and security; and (4) promoting opportunities and development. Sub-Saharan Africa is now home to 6 of the 10 fastest growing markets in the world. The IMF forecasts continued strong growth in the region.[21] There are broad based opportunities for American companies to deepen their trade and investment ties, including in the energy, agriculture, information, information and communications technology, and infrastructure sectors. To advance support and advance the U.S. Strategy, several senior government officials visited the region in the summer of 2012, with more visits this fall, including a Department of Commerce-led trade mission to South Africa and Zambia during November 26-30, 2012. In addition to pursuing new trade policy initiatives to promote and accelerate regional economic integration and enhanced trade facilitation efforts, a new Africa TPCC working group has been established to develop a "Doing Business in Africa" (DBIA) Campaign. The campaign will coordinate interagency efforts to better promote trade and investment opportunities in Sub-Saharan Africa, including efforts to mobilize the U.S. African Diaspora community.

Attract and Retain More Investment with SelectUSA

Located within the Department of Commerce, SelectUSA is a U.S. Government-wide initiative that leverages U.S. Commercial Service and other U.S. embassy and consulate personnel to attract and retain inbound investment in the United States to create and support American jobs. Increasing investment in the United States, through programs like SelectUSA, is crucial to growing the economy and creating jobs.

---

21 International Monetary Fund, Regional Economic Outlook: Sub-Saharan Africa, October 2012. http://www.imf.org/external/pubs/ft/reo/2012/afr/eng/sreo1012.htm

SelectUSA is the single point of contact at the national level to help international and domestic firms grow and invest in the United States. It serves as a strong partner to Economic Development Organizations (EDOs) in the United States that are looking to attract business investment.

SelectUSA coordinates business investment–related resources across all agencies of the U.S. Government. The initiative provides comprehensive information on establishing and operating a business, information on federal programs and services available—including grants, loans, and other assistance programs—and information on the competitive and regulatory landscape of doing business in the United States. SelectUSA exercises complete geographic neutrality and represents the entire United States.

SelectUSA is aggressively focused on attracting and retaining foreign direct investment (FDI) in the United States. The total stock of FDI in the United States is valued at more than $2.3 trillion, and preliminary data indicate that the United States received $220 billion worth of FDI in 2011 alone. These investments support U.S. jobs and the economy. Foreign-owned companies operating in the United States support more than 5.3 million U.S. jobs. Additionally, U.S. subsidiaries of foreign-owned firms account for 21 percent of all U.S. exports.

SelectUSA serves as the following:

- A Counselor: SelectUSA helps connect potential investors with EDOs in U.S. cities, states, and regions. It provides investors and EDOs with information on federal programs and services available to businesses operating in the United States—including grants, loans, and other assistance programs. As subject-matter experts, SelectUSA staff members help EDOs successfully attract and retain investment. For example, SelectUSA can share best practices with EDOs on how to improve their own FDI attraction efforts and create and implement an investment strategy, using data available at the Department of Commerce and other information sources.

- A Promoter and Global Platform: Through the Single Location Promotion Program, SelectUSA develops tailor-made events and marketing strategies in an effort to promote individual U.S. jurisdictions as FDI destinations. SelectUSA is part of ITA's U.S. Commercial Service, which has offices in over 70 countries around the world. In coordination with SelectUSA, trained U.S. Commercial Service staff can draw upon their market knowledge and business relationships to develop a customized scope of services—including business/government meetings, briefings, events, and other activities—to support state, regional, and local market promotion efforts.

- An Ombudsman: SelectUSA works to address issues involving federal rules, regulations, programs, or activities related to existing, pending, and potential investments. Working with SelectUSA, EDOs and investors can develop a better understanding of how to navigate U.S. regulations.

- An Advocate: U.S. cities, states, and regions have a strong legacy of pursuing and winning business investment projects. SelectUSA helps level the playing field for U.S. EDOs competing with foreign locations for new FDI. With SelectUSA, EDOs now have an advocate at the national level to help attract, retain, and grow investment in the United States.

The Department of Commerce is represented on the federal Interagency Investment Working Group (IIWG). The IIWG is convened and chaired by SelectUSA's Executive Director, in coordination with the Director of the National Economic Council. The IIWG consists of senior officials from: the Departments of State, the Treasury, Defense, Justice, Interior, Agriculture, Commerce, Labor, Veterans Affairs, Health and Human Services, Housing and Urban Development, Transportation, Energy, Education, and Homeland Security, the Environmental Protection Agency, SBA, Ex-Im Bank, the Office of the United States Trade Representative (USTR), the Domestic Policy Council, the National Economic Council, the National Security Staff, the Office of Management and Budget, and the Council of Economic Advisers, as well as such additional executive departments, agencies, and offices as the Secretary of Commerce may designate. The IIWG coordinates activities to promote business investment and respond to specific issues that affect business investment decisions. On average, the IIWG convenes quarterly.

The Administration's FY 2013 Trade Promotion Budget

The Federal Government is improving performance and making progress toward accomplishing NEI objectives with existing resources. However, as competition for new global middle-class consumers, major infrastructure projects, and inward investments intensifies, support for achieving the NEI's goals for U.S. exports and the jobs they support calls for new resources in some discrete areas.

The President's FY 2013 budget seeks the following:

- Department of Commerce: $30.3 million to expand the U.S. and Foreign Commercial Service's overseas export promotion activities and $12.3 million to implement the SelectUSA program of promoting business investment in the United States by foreign and domestic sources.

- SBA: Support for SBA's Office of International Trade to leverage SBA's business loan programs to finance exports. SBA's export finance and counseling were greatly enhanced by the passage of the Small Business Jobs Act, which increased the maximum size of export loan guarantees and expanded SBA's network of export finance specialists.

- Other core TPCC agencies: an increase of $19 million over 2012 levels for the Ex-Im Bank, U.S. Trade and Development Agency, USTR, the U.S. International Trade Commission, and the Overseas Private Investment Corporation.

Chapter 4:
NEI Progress Metrics

Economic Snapshot: Macroeconomic Metrics Show Steady Progress

Many factors beyond the control of the Federal Government can impact U.S. exports, including global market demand and currency fluctuations. Nevertheless, keeping abreast of the nation's export performance is an important guidepost to the Trade Promotion Coordinating Committee (TPCC) agencies' efforts. During the five-year term of the National Export Initiative (NEI), from 2009 through 2014, the TPCC has selected the following two measures to be used to track the export performance of the U.S. economy in terms of both dollars and business participation:[22]

Measure	2009	2010	2011
Value of exports ($ trillion)	$1.579	$1.842	$2.103
Percentage change from previous year	-14.3%	16.7%	14.2%

Measure	2009	2010
Number of U.S. exporting companies, total[22]	276,643	293,131
Percentage change from previous year	-4.5%	6.0%

NEI Progress Metrics

With respect to the management and oversight of the NEI, the TPCC now has a comprehensive set of interagency NEI progress metrics that are based on the programs, services, and initiatives of the TPCC agencies. These metrics measure the Federal Government's overall impact, rather than highlighting individual agencies' successes. Building on baseline numbers from the 2011 National Export Strategy (NES), the 2012 NES provides, for the first time, a clear year-over-year picture for most programs in which the U.S. Government has made progress since beginning implementation of the NEI in January 2010. In some key instances as noted, agencies have established new reporting channels with their public-private partners that have enabled them to begin aggregating these results with other agencies.

Strengthen Advocacy and Export Promotion

Small- and medium-sized enterprises (SMEs) face resource and market access hurdles that can limit their ability to participate in global trade. In particular, SMEs face insufficient knowledge of foreign markets in contrast with larger firms' access to market intelligence or direct presence in targeted foreign markets. SMEs also may not have the same capability as multinational companies to meet foreign buyers, address trade barriers, and manage risk. It is important for the Federal Government to meet the needs of exporters in critical areas that cannot be adequately addressed by the private sector. Sometimes, the Federal Government also advocates for U.S. companies that compete with aggressive foreign competitors, particularly on major foreign government procurements.

Prior to the publication of the 2011 NES, the TPCC developed the following measures in close consultation with the trade agencies. Agreed on definitions and timeframes were communicated to each agency, including a decision to base metrics on the calendar year given the January 2010 start date of the NEI. In some cases (e.g., in the Department of Commerce's [DOC] case), agencies are reporting on directly verified export transactions facilitated by Federal Government assistance. In other instances (e.g., in the case of the Small Business Administration [SBA] and the U.S. Department of Agriculture [USDA]), agencies are reporting on a combination of their own direct reporting and the reporting of resource partners such as the Small Business Development Centers (SBDCs)(affiliated with SBA) or the State Regional Trade Groups (affiliated with USDA).

22 U.S. Department of Commerce, U.S. Census Bureau, "A Profile of U.S. Importing and Exporting Companies, 2009–2010," April 12, 2012

Broaden and deepen SME exporting

The first priority of the NEI calls on the Federal Government to "develop programs designed to enhance export assistance to SMEs." SMEs are the backbone of the economy and of job creation. They also account for a growing share of overall U.S. exports. Yet, these companies face hurdles that limit their ability to participate in the global market (e.g., limited access to information and financing). The NEI priority to enhance export assistance to SMEs focuses on two distinct target SME populations: SMEs that are new to exporting and SMEs that are new to market. Both segments are critical to broadening and deepening U.S. exports. In the short term, the biggest boost to exports can come from encouraging current exporters to expand to new markets. However, in the long term, the U.S. Government must also encourage more companies to become exporters.

Number of new-to-export U.S. companies.

The TPCC agencies work closely through their own business counseling networks with public and private sector organizations. These counseling networks identify and assist firms with export potential. The USDA, for example, relies primarily on State Regional Trade Groups to reach out to SMEs. SBA began reporting on this measure in 2011, including the increasingly important role of its resource partners (SBDCs, Women's Business Centers [WBC], and SCORE) in assisting new-to-export companies. In close cooperation with SBA, the Department of Commerce's International Trade Administration (ITA) shifted its focus from new-to-export companies. This shift explains the drop in its new-to-export companies reported in the next measure below. These numbers are only a small subset of the companies helped by these agencies, including only companies that achieved a first successful export transaction with the U.S. Government's help.

Measure	2010	2011	Change	Agency
	406	211	-48%	DOC
# of new-to-export U.S. companies	627	1,403	NA[23]	USDA
	NA	129	NA	SBA
	1,033	1,743	NA	Total

Number of new markets entered by U.S. companies.

Of all the U.S. companies that export, 58 percent export to only one market and another 25 percent export to only two to four markets.[24] Especially in the short term, unleashing the country's export potential calls for encouraging companies to expand to new markets. The Department of Commerce ITA's New to Market Exporter Initiative directly targets companies that export to only one market. USDA has expanded its measure to include its export program partners, and SBA has laid the groundwork for reporting on this measure next year. These numbers are only a small subset of the companies helped by these agencies, including only new markets where companies achieved a first successful export transaction.

Measure	2010	2011	Change	Agency
	3,554	3,936	11%	DOC
# of new markets entered by U.S. companies	979	2,686	NA[25]	USDA
	4,533	6,622	NA	Total

Number of public-private partners and business counselors trained on exporting.

Collectively, public-private partners of the TPCC agencies represent tremendous "reach" into the SME business community. SBA's Resource Partners, for example, include 1,000 SBDCs, 100 WBCs, and 11,500 SCORE volunteers. The Export-Import Bank of the United States (Ex-Im Bank) resource partners include 67 City-State Partners. The U.S. Trade and Development Agency's (USTDA) Making Global Local initiative, which was just launched in May 2012, already includes 17 partner organizations

---

23 2011 data are a new expanded series that includes companies from all USDA export program partners.
24 The U.S. Census Bureau, "A Profile of U.S. Importing and Exporting Companies, 2009–2010," Exhibit 4a, April 12, 2012.
25 2011 data are a new expanded series that includes companies from all USDA export program partners.

across the country. By training partners such as these to talk to their clients about exporting and about export promotion resources available to them, TPCC agencies can dramatically expand their ability to engage SMEs. Given the intensified focus on training counselors and multipliers in "Chapter 2: The EPC's Plan for Maximizing the Effectiveness of Federal Programs," the TPCC expects these numbers to increase significantly in 2012.

Measure	2010	2011	Change	Agency
# of public-private partners and business counselors trained on exporting	200 business counselors	571 business counselors	149%	SBA[26]
	2,693 multipliers	1,161 multipliers	-57%	Ex-Im Bank[27]
	120 TPCC agency staff members	119 TPCC agency staff members	-1%	DOC
	3,013	1,851	-39%	Total

Number of new registrants on Export.gov.

Export.gov, which will be re-launched in early 2013 as part of the BusinessUSA family, serves as the Federal Government's one-stop shop for U.S. companies seeking information and resources on exporting. Under the NEI, all agencies are encouraging companies to visit Export.gov to access information. The number of Export.gov registrants, therefore, is a measure of the success of U.S. Government outreach efforts. Export.gov registration is also an increasingly important means by which companies are identifying themselves as interested in Federal Government export assistance.

Measure	2010	2011	Change	Agency
# of new registrants on Export.gov	5,373 U.S. organization registrants	6,972 U.S. organization registrants	30%	Reported by DOC

Dollar value of exports supported by counseling.

A typical SME may take 18 months to graduate from an interest in exporting to export success. SMEs can benefit tremendously from counseling to develop international business plans and market-entry strategies. At the same time, counseling can help experienced exporters to more effectively penetrate or enter new markets. In a major improvement to this metric, SBA began reporting in 2011 on the export results of counseling from several affiliated sources, including its U.S. Export Assistance Centers and District Offices, as well as its Resource Partners (including SBDCs, WBCs, and SCORE).

Measure	2010	2011	Change	Agency
$ value of exports supported by counseling	$1.15 billion	$2.83 billion	146%	DOC
	NA	$436 million	NA	SBA
Total (see grand total for trade promotion)	$1.15 billion	$3.27 billion	NA	Subtotal

Expand business facilitation programs

The NEI calls for agencies to promote federal resources that are currently available. The Federal Government can facilitate foreign market entry through a variety of export assistance programs. SMEs, in particular, are less likely to have a direct presence in foreign markets, and, therefore, are looking for convenient, affordable, yet high-impact opportunities to directly meet foreign buyers. The Commerce Department, for most industrial sectors, and USDA, for its part, lead these efforts. Through the NEI, these programs are now more strategically targeted (for example, to priority markets), are available to more U.S. companies, and include the participation of more TPCC agencies.

---

26 SBA data represent export training provided to field-based staff of TPCC agencies' Resource Partners (e.g., SBDC's WBCs, MEP Centers, Minority Business Centers, etc.), as well as city, state, and federal counseling entities.

27 Ex-Im multipliers include all non-exporting entities reached through speaking engagements that can assist in getting exporters to use Ex-Im Bank products (e.g., SBDCs, District Export Councils, Manufacturing Extension Partnerships, municipalities, universities, and fellow TPCC agencies).

Foreign trade missions.

Trade missions give both SMEs and larger firms direct access to foreign government decision makers and business contacts. NEI initiatives include targeting key emerging markets and enlisting more senior officials to lead missions. The Commerce Department's ITA has increased the number and average size of trade missions, as well as the intensity of follow-up with participants. As recruitment goals and interagency support increase, the TPCC agencies see growth in the:

- Number of U.S. companies participating in foreign trade missions
- Dollar value of exports resulting from foreign trade missions[28]

Measure	2010	2011	Change	Agency
# of U.S. companies participating in foreign trade missions	465 companies	557 companies	20%	DOC
	29 companies	57 companies	97%	USDA[28]
	6 companies	0 companies	-100%	DOT/SLSDC
	500	614	22%	Total
$ value of exports resulting from foreign trade missions	$47 million	$1.2 billion	2,300%	DOC
	$15 million	$15 million	0%	USDA
Total (see grand total for trade promotion)	$62 million	$1.2 billion	1,900%	Subtotal

Foreign buyer delegations.

Foreign buyer demand for "Made in the USA" is strong. Yet, the cost of meeting foreign buyers abroad can be too great for many SMEs. Therefore, several agencies bring foreign buyers to the United States to meet with U.S. goods and services producers. In 2011, Department of Commerce expanded its International Buyer Program, bringing thousands of foreign buyers to U.S. trade shows where U.S. SMEs were exhibiting. USTDA has increased the number of reverse trade missions of major foreign buyers (both public and private sector) by visiting cities across the United States to meet U.S. companies and visit manufacturing sites and facilities. These initiatives are resulting in a greater:

- Number of foreign public and private sector representatives brought to the United States
- Dollar value of exports resulting from foreign buyers

Measure	2010	2011	Change	Agency
# of foreign buyers brought to the U.S.	12,953	13,492	4%	DOC
	2,734	2,437	-3%	USDA[29]
	300 foreign delegates	600 foreign delegates	100%	USTDA[30]
	155 (approx.)	130	-16%	State[31]
	16,142	16,659	3%	Total
$ value of exports resulting from foreign buyers	$818 million	$901 million	10%	DOC[32]
Total (see grand total for trade promotion)	$818 million	$901 million	10%	Subtotal

28 USDA-led foreign trade missions; does not include missions led by USDA export program partners.
29 Buyers brought to the United States by USDA and export program partners.
30 Participants in more than 40 reverse trade missions are measured.
31 Data are based on Business Facilitation Incentive Fund Projects (the International Buyer Program or Regional Trade Shows).
32 Data are based on the International Buyer Program.

Foreign trade shows.

For export-ready companies, participating in a major foreign trade show is one of the fastest ways to increase exports. The Department of Commerce and USDA are strengthening their marketing and promotion of key trade events that offer matchmaking potential for SMEs. Both SBA and the Ex-Im Bank staffs have increased their participation in foreign trade shows, where they advise SME companies on trade financing. Although Department of Commerce ITA-supported shows included fewer participating companies in 2011, ITA achieved a greater number and value of export successes for these companies.

- Number of U.S. companies assisted at foreign trade shows
- Dollar value of exports resulting from foreign trade shows

Measure	2010	2011	Change	Agency
# of U.S. companies supported at foreign trade shows	3,799	2,699	-29%	DOC
	976	1,079	11%	USDA[33]
	2	4	100%	DOT/SLSDC
	4,777	3,782	21%	Total
$ value of exports resulting from foreign trade shows	$384 million	$10.5 billion	2,634%	DOC
	$1.07 billion	$1.12 billion	5%	USDA
Total (see grand total for trade promotion)	$1.45 billion	$11.62 billion	701%	Subtotal

Customized services.

Many companies need more customized market-entry assistance. Often, the company has done its homework, targeting a specific foreign market, and now needs more company- and product-specific market intelligence, or direct introductions to foreign buyers interested in their product (for example, Gold Key Service). As the TPCC agencies have expanded their customized solutions for SME exporters, there have been increases in the:

- Number of U.S. companies using customized services
- Dollar value of exports resulting from customized services

Measure	2010	2011	Change	Agency
# of U.S. companies using customized services	1,920	2,385	24%	DOC
	670	1,590	137%	USDA[34]
	25	53	112%	State
	2,615	4028	54%	Total
$ value of exports resulting from customized services	$2.09 billion	$3.33 billion	60%	DOC
Total (see grand total for trade promotion)	$2.09 billion	$3.33 billion	60%	Subtotal

Grand total for trade promotion

As the TPCC agencies have improved their services and conducted more outreach to U.S. companies, there has been a significant overall increase in the combined dollar value of exports supported by all the business facilitation activities listed earlier.

Measure	2010	2011	Change	
$ value of all trade promotion measures	$6.35 billion	$20.3 billion	211%	Grand Total[35]

---

33 Data are only for trade shows endorsed by USDA.
34 Does not include support provided directly to businesses by USDA export program partners.
35 2011 data include dollar value subtotals for Counseling ($3.27 billion), Foreign Trade Missions ($1.2 billion), Foreign Buyer Delegations ($901 million), Foreign Trade Shows ($11.62 billion), and Customized Services ($3.33 billion).

Provide on-the-ground commercial diplomacy support

When foreign governments adopt laws, regulations, or policies that make it more difficult for U.S. businesses to export or are unresponsive to requests from U.S. organizations, the U.S. Government's diplomatic corps in U.S. Embassies and Consulates abroad provide on-the-ground commercial diplomacy support on behalf of U.S. interests.

Measure	2010	2011	Change	Agency
$ value of commercial diplomacy successes	$4.2 billion	$16.7 billion	298%	DOC

Increase project advocacy wins

Project advocacy is a critical NEI priority given the rise of new competitors such as China and Brazil and the continued fierce competition from traditional export powerhouses such as Germany, Japan, and France. Emerging and developing countries are growing at a faster pace than in recent decades, along with demand for major infrastructure projects and other public-sector procurements. Given the horizontal nature of the U.S. Government (with multiple agencies involved in industry-related technical assistance, financing, and promotion), interagency program integration and Cabinet-level collaboration on these projects drives the TPCC agencies' success on behalf of U.S. industry, including SME bidders and SME suppliers to U.S. equipment manufacturers. As co-chair of the TPCC Advocacy Working Group with the State Department and as the parent agency of the Advocacy Center, ITA is working to drive increases in the:

- Number of advocacy wins: signed contracts as reported by firms working with the Advocacy Center on specific projects

- Dollar value of advocacy wins: U.S. export content as reported by the firm over the life of the contract

Measure	2010	2011	Change	Agency
# advocacy wins (total)	46	53	15%	Advocacy Center
$ value of advocacy wins (U.S. export content)	$18.7 billion	$23.9 billion	33%	Total

Provide Greater Access to Export Financing

The NEI calls on the trade finance agencies (primarily Ex-Im Bank, SBA, and the USDA Foreign Agricultural Service) to increase the availability of export financing to SMEs. For many U.S. exporters, public-sector financing is crucial to their ability to effectively finance their export-related activities and to compete in foreign markets. This has been especially true since the recent financial crisis, because banks and other financial services firms curtailed their lending and risk-taking capacities. Therefore, U.S. Government agencies have sought to make more financing available, consistent with U.S. obligations under international agreements, through existing financing platforms and new products that address the shortage in financing capacity in the private sector.

Overall trade financing levels.

To address the financing challenges faced by businesses, the U.S. Government achieved increases in the:

- Dollar value of exports supported
- Number of transactions supported

Measure	2010	2011	Change	Agency
$ value of exports supported	$32.5 billion	$38.1 billion	17%	Ex-Im Bank
	$1.0 billion	$1.84 billion	84%	SBA
	$3.3 billion	$4.24 billion	28%	USDA
	$36.8 billion	$44.18 billion	20%	Total
# of transactions supported	3,589	3,752	5%	Ex-Im Bank
	1,473	1,509	2%	USDA
	5,062	5,261	4%	Total

Small business financing.

Agencies are expanding the eligibility criteria for lending to small businesses and streamlining application and review processes for small businesses. Ex-Im Bank offers Express Insurance, a supply chain finance guarantee, a reinsurance product, and Renewable Energy Express. The Small Business Jobs Act raised the maximum size of SBA's International Trade Loans, Export Working Capital Loans, and Export Express Loans. Improvements in processes, limits, and outreach are increasing the dollar value of small business exports supported. SBA and Ex-Im Bank are reaching out to more community banks in partnership with the Treasury Department's Office of the Comptroller of the Currency and the Federal Reserve District Banks.

- Number of small business exporters assisted by U.S. Government finance programs
- Dollar value of small business exports supported
- Number of lenders trained

Measure	2010	2011	Change	Agency
# of small exporters assisted by U.S. Government finance programs	2,586	2,550	-1%	Ex-Im Bank
	1,082 (1,216 loans)	1055 (1,191 loans)	-2%	SBA
	3,668	3605	-2%	Total
$ value of small firm exports supported	$10.3 billion	$12.2 billion	18%	Ex-Im Bank
	$1.0 billion	$1.84 billion	84%	SBA
	$11.3 billion	$14.04 billion	24%	Total
# lenders trained (individuals)	729	717	-2%	Ex-Im Bank
	3,804	3,332	-12%	SBA
	4,533	4,049	-11%	Total

Reduce Trade Barriers and Enforce Trade Rules

A key approach to expanding U.S. exports and thus supporting American jobs is through enhanced market access and the reduction of foreign government–imposed barriers to trade. Consequently, the Office of the U.S. Trade Representative (USTR) leads the U.S. Government's continued focus, in the NEI context, on efforts to spur exports by opening markets through new trade and investment agreements, effectively using existing trade agreements and trade policy forums to address and remove trade barriers, and, where necessary, pursuing robust enforcement of trade agreements and U.S. trade laws.

Concluding trade agreements.

- In 2011, the Administration secured Congressional approval of three market-opening trade agreements with Korea, Colombia, and Panama, with significant, anticipated benefits for U.S. exporters. The United States–Korea Free Trade Agreement entered into force on March 15, 2012, the United States–Colombia Trade Promotion Agreement entered into force on May 15, 2012, and the United States–Panama Trade Promotion Agreement entered into force on October 31, 2012. The United States is already seeing increased exports of goods and services into these markets.

  With Korea's $1.2 trillion economy and a bilateral trade relationship totaling more than $100 billion in 2011, the U.S.-Korea trade agreement is the United States' most commercially significant trade pact in 18 years. According to the U.S. International Trade Commission, full elimination of tariffs on goods exports alone is expected to increase annual U.S. exports by up to $11 billion. The agreement also further opens Korea's $580 billion services market to U.S. exports and investment, addresses regulatory and other non-tariff barriers, and strengthens protection of intellectual property rights. All of these measures will help U.S. businesses sell more goods and services in Korea, which will support higher-paying jobs in the United States.

- The United States and the eight other Trans-Pacific Partnership (TPP) members agreed in late 2011 on the broad outlines for an ambitious, state-of-the-art TPP agreement that will enhance trade and investment among the TPP countries, promote innovation, increase economic growth and development, and support the creation and retention of jobs in America and around the Asia-Pacific region. This agreement will create significant new opportunities to increase U.S. exports that support higher-paying jobs in the United States. The Asia-Pacific region includes some of the world's most dynamic economies, representing more than 40 percent of global trade. The region is already a key destination for U.S. manufactured goods, agricultural products, and services. In 2011, the region accounted for more than 60 percent of U.S. goods exports and nearly three-quarters of U.S. total agricultural exports. Canada and Mexico have joined the TPP negotiations as of early October 2012, following the successful conclusion of the domestic procedures of each of the current TPP countries for addition of new participants, which will generate even more opportunities for U.S. export growth, allow U.S. companies to leverage their existing North American supply chains by exporting goods to other TPP countries.

- In November 2011, the United States and the Philippines signed a customs administration and trade facilitation agreement, which includes specific commitments on trade facilitation, including on simplified customs procedures and transparency of customs administration, which will promote increased bilateral trade.

- At the November 19, 2012 U.S.-ASEAN Leaders Meeting in Phnom Penh, President Obama and Association of Southeast Asia Nations (ASEAN) Leaders launched the U.S.-ASEAN Expanded Economic Engagement (E3) initiative, a new framework for economic cooperation designed to expand trade and investment ties and create new business opportunities and jobs in all eleven countries. In addition, by working together on E3 initiatives, many of which correspond to specific issues addressed in trade agreements, the U.S. and ASEAN will lay the groundwork for ASEAN countries to prepare to join high-standard trade agreements such as the Trans-Pacific Partnership (TPP) agreement that the United States is currently negotiating with ten countries in Asia and the Western Hemisphere. E3 complements the ambitious 2013 Trade and Investment Framework Agreement (TIFA) Work plan that United States Trade Representative Ron Kirk and ASEAN Economic Ministers concluded at the U.S.-ASEAN Economic Ministers Meeting and Business Summit in August 2012. The new TIFA agenda includes a proposed ASEAN Economic Ministers Road Show to the United States, plans for a second U.S.-ASEAN Business Summit following the success of this year's Summit, cooperation on principles governing Information and Communication Technology, support for Small and Medium Enterprises, and work on services, trade and the environment, standards, and trade facilitation.

Using existing trade agreements and trade policy forums.

The mere existence of a trade agreement does not ensure that expected benefits will flow to U.S. exporters, investors, and workers. Accordingly, the TPCC agencies focus their attention equally on ensuring that existing trade agreements are being adequately used by U.S. exporters and that opportunities are pursued to reduce barriers to exports in a wide variety of ongoing trade policy forums and dialogues. USTR achieves considerable progress in expanding U.S. export opportunities each year under existing frameworks such as various Free Trade Commission meetings, TIFAs, and other regional and bilateral forums. The more than 20 World Trade Organization (WTO) standing committees provide an effective forum for the United States to raise and resolve WTO trade compliance issues with other WTO trading partners before such issues rise to the level of a formal dispute. Key examples are presented in Appendix A on NEI recommendation updates. However, it is very difficult to aggregate this progress into a single metric.

- USTR's work to prevent and remove unjustified foreign sanitary and phytosanitary (SPS) and technical barriers serves President Obama's goal of doubling American exports by the end of 2014 through the NEI. USTR's Report on Sanitary and Phytosanitary (SPS) Barriers to Trade focuses on unjustified SPS barriers that block American agricultural exports. The report also outlines the increasing opportunities for American agricultural products abroad, such as the removal of China's ban on live swine from the United States. USTR's Report on Technical Barriers to Trade (TBT), addresses unwarranted or overly burdensome technical barriers that make it difficult for American manufacturers and workers to sell their products abroad. These new tools were developed through increased coordination between USTR and the Departments of State, Labor, Commerce, and Agriculture, and other federal agencies to spot and respond more quickly and effectively when U.S. trading partners fail to meet their obligations under trade agreements to which the United States is a party.

For example, the TBT report released since the 2011 NES describes an agreement the United States reached with the European Union (EU) to allow organic products certified in the United States or in the EU to be sold as organic in either market. This partnership between the world's two largest organic producers will promote the growing American organic industry and support U.S. jobs and businesses. The SPS and TBT reports are released in conjunction with the 2012 National Trade Estimate (NTE) Report on Foreign Trade Barriers, which identifies significant foreign barriers to U.S. exports of goods and services, U.S. foreign direct investment, and the protection of intellectual property rights and outlines the actions the Obama Administration has taken to reduce or eliminate those barriers, which serves the objective of the NEI. The NTE Report covers policies in almost 90 foreign markets.

The USDA compliance program includes technical interventions involving information exchange between U.S. and foreign regulatory agencies; technical assistance through targeted capacity building programs; and formal or informal diplomatic interventions.

- One important area in which detailed statistics are collected and reported involves the ITA's Trade Agreement Compliance Program. ITA leads a process of working with individual firms or business groups to identify barriers to exports (which can involve USTR, USDA, and Department of State resources as well). Once identified, teams of experts use the leverage of existing trade agreements to seek removal of the barrier in question. ITA closely tracks its progress in expanding export opportunities through this casework.

Measure	2010	2011	Change	Agency
# of compliance and market access cases initiated	219 cases, 89 on behalf of SMEs	246 cases, 88 on behalf of SMEs	12%	DOC/ITA
# of compliance and market access cases successfully resolved	82 barriers in 45 different markets	91 barriers in 45 different markets	11%	DOC/ITA
# of foreign measures reviewed and addressed with U.S. stakeholders	282 measures in 50 different countries	285 measures in 52 different countries	1%	USDA/FAS
$ value of U.S. markets preserved through resolving foreign market access measures	$2.3 billion for 33 issues	$3.9 billion for 41 issues	70%	USDA/FAS

Pursuing robust enforcement

USTR, working with USDA and ITA, has been active and forceful in its use of formal dispute settlement processes to pursue foreign trade barriers that have a significant negative impact on exports of U.S. products. Although it is difficult to arrive at a common metric across all of these dispute-settlement actions, several examples are cited in the NEI recommendations update in Appendix A. In addition, with the establishment of the Interagency Trade Enforcement Center, the Administration will have more resources available to investigate, and if necessary pursue, any country's failure to abide by international trade rules and commitments.

Enforcing U.S. trade laws

ITA's and CBP's robust enforcement of the U.S. antidumping and countervailing duty laws helps level the playing field for U.S. exporters by providing U.S. industries with a reliable mechanism to remedy market distortions caused by unfair trade practices that can undermine a company's global competitiveness. ITA also advocates on behalf of U.S. exporters subject to foreign trade remedy actions, working to ensure that U.S. exports are not unjustly restricted in the process.[36]

---

36 Metrics for these latter two enforcement practices are available and can be reported.

Appendix A:

Tracking Progress on the September 2010 NEI Recommendations

NEI Recommendations Update

In March 2010, President Obama issued an Executive Order outlining the priorities of the National Export Initiative (NEI) and establishing the first-ever Export Promotion Cabinet (EPC).[37] The Executive Order directed the EPC, through the Trade Promotion Coordinating Committee (TPCC), to develop recommendations for implementing eight NEI priority areas of activity, which the EPC did in a Report to the President delivered in September 2010. Since then, the TPCC's annual National Export Strategy Report to Congress (NES) has reported on the progress of the original 70 recommendations the Export Promotion Cabinet made in September 2010. The June 2011 National Export Strategy Report covered these recommendations in both a highlights chapter and an appendix accounting for each recommendation. Similarly, the 2012 annual report provides highlights of priority accomplishments in this appendix or in "Chapter 1: NEI Accomplishments to Date and Follow-up on Priority Initiatives."

The March 2010 Executive Order identified eight NEI priority areas of activity:

- Priority 1: Exports by Small and Medium-Sized Enterprises (SMEs)
- Priority 2: Federal Export Assistance
- Priority 3: Trade Missions
- Priority 4: Commercial Advocacy
- Priority 5: Increasing Export Financing
- Priority 6: Macroeconomic Rebalancing
- Priority 7: Reducing Barriers to Trade
- Priority 8: Export Promotion of Services

The 70 recommendations cover all major components of these eight priority areas under the NEI, cut across many Federal Government agencies, and focus on areas where concerted Federal Government efforts can help increase exports.

---

37   Executive Order 13534, March 11, 2010.

Priority 1: Exports by SMEs

The Federal Government can encourage and facilitate SME exports by raising public awareness of export opportunities and available assistance and by directing export promotion and financing services to address the changing needs of exporters. TPCC agencies continue to realign their programs and services to more effectively identify, prepare, connect, and support SME exporters.

Identify SMEs that can begin or expand exporting.

Recommendation	Status and Next Steps
Conduct a National Outreach Campaign.	
a. A redesigned Export.gov website to help new-to-export and new-to-market businesses.	Export.gov 2.0: The NEI's ambitious goal of doubling exports calls for a next generation web platform that serves U.S. exporters' needs as they seek to expand internationally. The Federal Government needs to serve increasingly larger numbers of companies to meet NEI goals. Service delivery via a content-rich, robust web portal is a critical piece of the strategy to meet increased demand from clients and to reach out to new firms. In addition, businesses expect to access information and contacts via a self-service web portal, then follow-up for individualized advice and higher-level counseling at a later stage in the process. In January 2013, Export.gov 2.0, a part of the BusinessUSA family, will begin to deliver personalized content to SMEs through a "MyExport.gov" type of experience. On the basis of a company's profile (including industry, exporting maturity, size of company, etc.), information on events, market research, and trade leads will be pushed to them. Export.gov 2.0 will make it easier for SMEs to do business with the U.S. Government by streamlining and auto-populating forms used to collect information. Export.gov 2.0 technology and service delivery will also deliver content and services to the BusinessUSA.gov platform seamlessly. Together, Export.gov 2.0 and BusinessUSA.gov will save SMEs valuable time and effort. Export Business Planner: The Small Business Administration (SBA) launched the online, interactive export business planner in June 2011. As of March 2012, the tool had been downloaded more than 4600 times, with nearly 10,000 unique page views. The tool is used regularly by SBDC counselors to work with clients. The Massachusetts Export Center conducted an experimental workshop in spring 2012 that walked participants through writing an international business plan using the SBA Export Business Planner.
b. An increased number of national outreach events.	As featured in Chapter 2 (p. 20), the EPC has established a 2012 goal of launching a national outreach campaign targeting SMEs. This national outreach strategy, currently under development, will expand on the national outreach initiatives reported in the 2011 NES ("New Markets, New Jobs" and "Small Business Global Access" conferences, and the "Take Your Business Global" educational video series produced in cooperation with Inc. Magazine and AT&T). The goal is to devise a national marketing campaign with public and private sector partners that raises baseline public awareness of exporting.
c. Advertising and direct mail campaign to increase SME awareness.	A productive partnership between TPCC agencies and the Department of Commerce's U.S. Census Bureau has resulted in a number of marketing initiatives targeting different market segments. The U.S. Census Bureau's semiannual "TradeSource" e-newsletter is written by the TPCC agencies and distributed by the U.S. Census Bureau to 100,000+ current exporters that use the U.S. Census Bureau's Automated Export System. TradeSource informs companies that are already exporting about new Federal Government programs and initiatives. The January 2012 edition focused entirely on programs of interest to services sector exporters. An additional outreach tool is a collection of 30 videos produced by the Department of Commerce's International Trade Administration (ITA) and the U.S. Census Bureau. The videos are hosted on YouTube and are accessible on multiple websites. Topics include foreign trade regulations, how to complete certificates of origin, and how to use publicly available export data to identify new markets. New videos are added periodically, and total views per year average about 100,000. In July 2012, the TPCC-Census partnership produced "The Exporter's Toolkit," a handy pocket-sized flipper designed to demystify exporting and the availability of export assistance from the Federal Government. The July 2012 special edition of the TradeSource e-newsletter is based on "The Exporter's Toolbox" (http://www.census.gov/foreign-trade/aes/tradesource_july2012.pdf). In partnership with the Bureau of Industry and Security and Customs and Border Protection, the U.S. Census Bureau has organized a series of Export Compliance Seminars nationally for companies ready to export. In 2012, the U.S. Census Bureau, SBA, and the Association of Small Business Development Centers (ASBDC) is organizing a series of "Go Global Export 101" seminars targeting companies that are new to exporting with training on using Federal Government trade data resources to explore and target foreign markets. The U.S. Census Bureau and the TPCC are including a "Why Export" flyer in the materials being mailed to more than 400,000 U.S. companies as part of the 2012 Economic Census. The flyer highlights that there is an opportunity for small businesses to look internationally for new markets and that the Federal Government has the resources to help small businesses be successful exporters.

The United States Department of Agriculture (USDA) provided $200,000 in additional funding to the State Regional Trade Groups (SRTG) for a training series entitled "Explore Exporting". Up to 20 seminars will provide essential export information to U.S. food and agricultural businesses. The seminars are in partnership with State Departments of Agriculture. Through July 2012, the SRTG's completed 17 seminars and reached 222 SMEs in 15 states The SRTG's also enhanced outreach to foreign buyers through updated websites, and newly designed marketing and promotional materials about upcoming events and available services. |
| **Coordinate, expand, and leverage federal outreach resources to identify potential exporters.** | The 2011 NES highlighted new interagency processes using companies' Export.gov registrations. In developing the next generation of Export.gov, the TPCC agencies are closely coordinating efforts to further improve client referral and self-help.

As noted in Chapter 2, the Export Promotion Cabinet is currently developing an interagency plan to maximize the impact of federal export promotion infrastructure, including global distribution networks, by bringing a customer-oriented focus to U.S. Government efforts. |
| **Increase collaboration with the private sector.** | SBA partnered with Visa to conduct the first-ever YouTube Small Business Export Success Story Contest that asked small businesses to share their exporting successes with others. The goal was to inform small businesses about the advantages of exporting and to increase awareness of Federal Government assistance available to support small business exporters through the first-person stories of successful entrepreneurs. There were 35 entries, with a total of 4,527 votes through YouTube and Facebook. Winners were announced at a ceremony at the District Export Council Annual Conference in Las Vegas, NV, on November 5, 2011. The next YouTube Export Video Contest is currently slated to be launched in January 2013, with contest winners to be awarded in late May or early June of 2013. |
| **Analyze existing research to better understand the types of SMEs that become successful exporters.** | Implemented: Agencies have integrated the market segmentation study into their internal processes and program outreach. |

Identify SMEs that can begin or expand exporting.

Recommendation	Status and Next Steps
Mine existing databases for outreach to prospects for trade facilitation support.	Database Mining: Because of privacy policy constraints, this recommendation has proven difficult to pursue at this time.

Prepare SMEs to export successfully.

Recommendation	Status and Next Steps
Enhance training resources on Export.gov.	Research on small and medium-sized exporting companies points to a steep learning curve on the road to making an initial export sale or expanding into new international markets. To make more readily available the information, knowledge, and skills needed by small companies to help them export faster and more profitably, Export.gov now offers a number of practical learning tools.

The first tool is A Basic Guide to Exporting. Now in its 10th edition with a new NEI version, all 17 chapters of the Basic Guide are now available via Export.gov. In addition, an e-book version of the Basic Guide is now available for purchase and for downloading to popular e-reader devices. For businesspeople on the move, Michigan State University has created podcast modules of each chapter for viewing and listening on portable devices (e.g., iTunes) under globalEDGE online course modules or at http://globaledge.msu.edu.

The book has generated a companion series of webinars. Also called "A Basic Guide to Exporting," the series features about 30 different titles ranging from how to write an Export plan to export opportunities in India. Recordings of these webinars are then hosted on Export.gov where they can be viewed at the convenience of visitors to the site. There have been about 30,000 downloads of the webinars during the past 6 months.

A series of webinars has also been delivered to strategic partners including United Parcel Service, Federal Express, the United States Postal Service, and a number of industry associations. Training sales professionals who interact daily with small businesses generates more exporting SMEs and more SME awareness of U.S. Government trade promotion services.

To make export expertise more widely available, SBA and the U.S. Commercial Service have teamed up to offer online export training to counselors of the SBDCs. The page, which is specifically designed for counselors, provides webinars and other resources and focuses on developing an introductory and intermediate-level competency in international trade. Counselors must pass an online exam to receive certification at those levels. Counselors with even minimal competency or exposure to international trade issues are more likely to raise the prospect of exporting with clients and be more aware of appropriate referral. |
Implement a program to "Train the Trainers."	
a. Institute TPCC International Trade Certificate Training for small business counselors.	In September 2011, two introductory workshops at the 2011 ASBDC conference averaged 120 participants. The five intermediate course offerings averaged 90 attendees, and five non-core international workshops averaged 50 attendees. The 2012 ASBDC conference had an even more aggressive international trade program. The Department of Commerce and SBA established a page on Export.gov to mirror the ASBDC training, providing access to webinars and other training resources for counselors who are not able to participate in the annual ASBDC conference training. The page also includes links to certification exams at the Introductory and Intermediate levels. Through the first half of 2012, more than 400 SBDC business counselors have taken and passed the introductory and intermediate certificate training tests on export counseling. SBA is also making reimbursements available though Small Business Jobs Act funds in 2012 for counselors to attend advanced Certified Global Business Professional accreditation, and funds permitting, SBA will sponsor training for additional counselors in 2013.
b. Use "Export Outreach Teams" to provide local small business counselors with exporting basics.	Following successful pilot events in Baltimore, MD, Washington DC, and Minneapolis, MN SBA U.S. Export Assistance Centers have the goal in 2012 of conducting one Export Outreach Workshop for every three District Offices they cover. These workshops bring small business counselors together with local international trade specialists to learn the basics of exporting, to discuss identifying export readiness in clients, and to understand where to turn to help clients take that next step to global market success.
Promote export opportunities among competitive industry clusters.	According to survey results from a year-one evaluation of SBA's 10 contract-based clusters, nearly 16 percent of small business respondents reported that they were able to increase their exports during the first year as a result of their cluster participation.
Prepare the Department of Commerce ITA's Trade Information Center to effectively direct prospective exporters to appropriate local resources.	With the planned next generation of Export.gov, the Trade Information Center is being transformed into a knowledge center that more effectively manages cross-governmental multimedia content for exporters.

Connect SMEs to export opportunities.

Recommendation	Status and Next Steps
Pilot an Export Intermediary Matchmaker program.	Export Intermediary Matchmaker: To promote the use of export management companies and export trading companies by small business manufacturers and suppliers, SBA conducted a pilot Export Matchmaker Trade Show and Conference in New Jersey in 2010. The event drew 165 participants. Because of that success the Agency conducted a Florida Edition Matchmaker 2011 which drew 216 participants. SBA plans to continue building the Export Matchmaker brand by conducting a Midwest Edition Matchmaker on October 22, 2012, in St. Louis, MO.
Develop export assistance packages that effectively combine the programs of various agencies.	Export Assistance Packages: Agencies continue to promote SBA's Export Express to companies participating in trade shows overseas and to finance costs of other U.S. Government export business development services. In addition, the SBA and the Export-Import Bank of the United States will do a joint promotion highlighting the benefits of combining the SBA's Export Express loan program with the Ex-Im Bank's Express Credit Insurance program.

Connect SMEs to export opportunities.

Recommendation	Status and Next Steps
Implement bilateral and multilateral SME-to-SME initiatives to connect U.S. SMEs to international business opportunities.	U.S.-European Union (EU) SME Best Practices Workshop: In 2011, the U.S. and EU launched the SME Best Practices workshops in Brussels and Washington to identify ways to address barriers and enhance SME participation in transatlantic trade, with continuing U.S.-EU cooperation in 2012. As a result of the SME workshops and stakeholder input, the United States and EU intend to conclude a Memorandum of Understanding (MOU) on SME trade promotion cooperation in 2012.
	SME Exporters Toolkit: In July 2012, the TPCC-Census partnership produced "The Exporter's Toolkit," a handy pocket-sized flipper designed to demystify exporting and the availability of export assistance from the Federal Government. The July 2012 special edition of the TradeSource e-newsletter is based on "The Exporter's Toolbox" (www.census.gov/foreign-trade/aes/tradesource_july2012.pdf).
	Free Trade Agreement (FTA) Tariff Tool: To help small businesses take better advantage of export opportunities under U.S. FTAs, TPCC agencies plan to update and expand the capabilities of the tool with user-friendly information for SMEs, including the addition of Rules of Origin, textiles, and agriculture tariffs.
	New FTAs: With the Congressional approval of the Korea, Colombia and Panama FTAs and the entry into force of the Korea FTA on March 15, the Colombia FTA on May 15, and the Panama FTA on October 31, agencies plan increased outreach to SMEs to raise awareness of important new opportunities in those markets.
	Linking SBDCs for international trade and Small Business Network of the Americas: SBA, the Office of the U.S. Trade Representative (USTR) and the State Department have engaged and supported the SBDCGlobal.com initiative linking SBDC clients in the United States, Mexico, and Central America to each other. The U.S. SBDC model is now expanding in Latin American countries including additional Central American countries, the Dominican Republic, Colombia, and Caribbean countries. The Small Business Network of the Americas, as announced by the White House in 2012, will connect SBDCs and similar small business support centers to encourage diaspora entrepreneurship and small business partnerships in the Western Hemisphere.
	Next Steps: Consider other markets for pilot project.

Support SMEs once they find export opportunities.

Recommendation	Status and Next Steps
Produce trade financing marketing materials that provide a clear and concise summary of all federal trade and investment financing programs.	In January 2011, the TPCC Small Business Working Group produced a brochure on U.S. Government exports and foreign investment finance programs for interagency outreach. The brochure will be updated by March 2013.
Provide trade finance counseling at major international trade shows.	SBA, Ex-Im Bank, and USDA Foreign Agricultural Service provided export finance counseling and training at 38 domestic industry shows and 7 international trade shows during FY2011 and are on schedule to provide similar counseling and training at 35 domestic International Buyer Program (IBP) shows and 9 international trade shows in FY2012—delivering timely on-the-ground support to U.S. SME exhibitors at these major events.
Train lenders in the U.S. Government's export finance programs.	To expand the delivery infrastructure for federal trade finance programs, SBA and Ex-Im Bank are collaborating with the Office of the Comptroller of the Currency (OCC) and the district offices of the Federal Reserve Bank to do more outreach and training of community banks. Over the past three fiscal years (2010-2012), this initiative has trained over six hundred community bank lenders. In November (FY 2013), SBA and Ex-Im Bank organized a webinar with OCC for 234 lenders, putting the agencies well on their way to achieving their goal of training 3,000 lenders by the end of CY 2015.
Develop "whole of government" financing packages to meet the needs of SME exporters and lenders alike.	The Ex-Im Bank, SBA, USDA Foreign Agricultural Service, and the Overseas Private Investment Corporation (OPIC) are working together to develop "Global Business Solutions" packages that are based on a "problem-solution" matrix, rather than agency-specific financing options. These packages will be developed during FY 2013 and pushed out to the lending community in an effort to breakdown the silos among agencies and address the needs of both the SME community and lenders who need to better understand how the various U.S. Government programs can meet their clients' needs.
Explore the feasibility of creating one set of performance measures that would apply to all the U.S. Government's export financing agencies.	Successfully implemented. The 2011 NES inaugurated cross-governmental finance and SME finance metrics. In addition, SBA and Ex-Im Bank are in the process of setting collaborative referral and performance goals for their staffs in FY 2013.

Priority 2: Federal Export Assistance

The Federal Government works with U.S. companies to help them enter foreign markets through a variety of export assistance programs that connect U.S. businesses to market opportunities. Federal Government agencies also have field-based staff members to connect prospective U.S. exporters with potential foreign buyers. The NEI contains a series of recommendations focusing on better coordinating U.S. Government assistance efforts as well as expanding the programs that increase opportunities that match foreign buyers with U.S. companies.

Short-Term Recommendations:

Recommendation	Status and Next Steps
Emphasize the New Market Exporter Initiative.	In 2012, ITA's Strategic Partnership Program continued to promote successful public-private partnership programs through the growth of the New Market Exporter Initiative (NMEI) and the introduction of the Global Buyers Initiative (GBI). The NMEI leverages strategic partners to expand U.S. exports by identifying their customers and members who sell to at least one international market and helping them sell to additional markets. The GBI was developed as a foreign buyer recruitment program to better identify and align foreign importers with U.S. exporters. The program seeks to leverage private sector and non-governmental organizations to identify their customers or members whose imports from the United States do not represent a majority of their purchases and to help those customers or members expand their sourcing from the United States. To date, the NMEI has 23 active partners and has generated more than 550 company registrations within the past year, while the GBI has developed initial partnerships with 16 organizations. Moreover, as these new partners begin their marketing efforts, the TPCC believes the initiative will achieve similar results. By using the NMEI to focus on small and medium-sized U.S. companies that are already knowledgeable about exporting and by using the GBI in identifying current foreign importers who are underserved, the TPCC will increase the likelihood of having the largest impact on U.S. exports. The Strategic Partnership Program has grown exponentially in 2012 from 18 public private partnership agreements to 96 agreements with companies and associations.
Recruit more potential foreign buyers to U.S. trade shows and create additional opportunities for partnerships.	In 2011, ITA's IBP recruited nearly 13,500 prospective buyers from international markets to come to participating U.S. trade events to meet U.S. exporters. As a result, the IBP helped generate more than $900 million in exports in 2011—a 10 percent increase over 2010. More than 49 percent of these successes were by U.S. firms that exported to a new market.

The comparative advantage of IBPs versus other business-to-business matchmaking service offerings is that they enable U.S. companies to meet a breadth of prospective buyers from around the world in one domestic venue. Thus, there is significant demand from U.S. trade show organizers to participate in the IBP. Over the past three years, the IBP has received an average of 70 applications annually. Between 2010 and 2012, the percentage of repeat applicants ranged from 61 percent to 72 percent, indicating strong customer satisfaction among U.S. trade show organizer clients.

In spite of strong demand from trade show organizers, and IBP's track record as one of the U.S. Commercial Service's biggest export success generators, the IBP had to reduce the number of shows it certified by more than 20 percent in 2012 because of capacity and funding constraints. To explore ways to increase the number of IBP venues in 2013, the U.S. Commercial Service plans to pilot a tiered IBP portfolio of services that would provide a range of service level options to trade show organizers according to the number of international delegates recruited to their shows.

USDA's network of overseas offices organized foreign buyer teams from 12 countries totaling 155 participants. In addition, USDA's export program partners organized 303 reverse trade missions bringing 2,437 foreign buyers to the United States to meet with suppliers, often in conjunction with domestic trade shows, with reported sales of $1.3 billion.

The Trade Fair Certification (TFC) Program has certified 98 events to date for 2012, 5 events more than in 2011. The TFC Program expects to certify a total of 110 events for 2012. The TFC program has played host to 1,500 U.S. companies at the 41 TFC events hosted to date in 2012.

Current TFC initiatives include the following:

• There are nine events scheduled for ITA Global Team member presence in 2012 to conduct value added services such as Showtime and business-to-business matchmaking appointments.

• ITA rolled out Business-to-Business Matchmaking Software at the AUTOMECHANIKA 2012 Exhibition in Frankfurt, Germany September 13–17, 2012.

• U.S. Commercial Service will collaborate with the Department of Defense's Office of Defense Cooperation at 10 overseas Aerospace and Defense exhibitions.

• SBA supported U.S. exhibitors at the GLOBE 2012, Hannover Messe 2012, and AUTOMECHANIKA 2012 exhibition by providing counseling on SBA and Ex-Im Bank trade financing programs.

Event Highlight:

Arab Health 2012, the largest medical products and services show in the Middle East (second only to Medica in the world), welcomed 200 U.S. exhibitors, including 150 in the USA Pavilion, of which 50 were exhibiting for the first time. Ambassador Michael Corbin and Acting Minister of Health HE Abdul Rahman Al Owais participated in the ribbon cutting ceremony. Multiple elements of the Department of Commerce contributed to a Showtime program; counseling services by Commercial Specialists from the United Arab Emirates, Qatar, Kuwait, Saudi Arabia (Riyadh and Dhahran), Oman, and Bahrain; a delegation of nine American hospitals under ITA's Market Development Cooperator Program; and U.S. exhibitor counseling services by the U.S. Census Bureau officers on using U.S. trade data. More than $20 million in export successes were recorded at the show.

USDA completed an internal pilot study to verify the accuracy of projected sales by trade show exhibitors for the 12-month period following the show. The study found actual sales as a whole exceed exhibitor projections. USDA also commissioned a third-party evaluation of its trade show program to develop recommendations for improving stakeholder service beginning in 2012. |

Short-Term Recommendations:

Recommendation	Status and Next Steps
Increase U.S. Government support for U.S. renewable energy and energy efficiency exports.	ITA released the first Renewable Energy and Efficiency Export Initiative (RE4I) Annual Review in October 2011, indicating that all of RE4I's 23 deliverables were either accomplished or in the process of implementation. Accomplishments include the following: • Led the first renewable energy trade policy roundtable under the RE4I, bringing 19 companies to Mexico for high-level discussions with the Mexican Government (led by Under Secretary Sánchez); • Created the Renewables Express program at Ex-Im Bank, streamlining the processing of renewable energy applications; • Made a $500 million supplemental call for investment proposals from OPIC to recapitalize six clean energy investment funds; • Completed a first-of-its-kind Renewable Energy Top Prospects Study to focus limited government resources on those markets and technologies most likely to result in U.S. exports over the NEI time frame; • Expanded the Green Embassies Program, which now includes more than 75 embassies and consulates around the world; • Led four renewable energy trade missions (India, South Africa, Turkey, and Saudi Arabia); • Contributed to a significant increase in renewable energy reverse trade missions organized by USTDA • Provided the first-ever support for biomass pellet market development activities through the USDA's Market Access Program • Developed a renewable energy and energy efficiency (RE&EE) exporters' portal on Export.gov that provides information on events, market research, and news from across the U.S. Government to RE&EE exporters • Developed a new OPIC financing program for leasing U.S.-made renewable energy equipment (key for geothermal drilling) and energy efficiency improvements

Expand opportunities for the U.S. civil nuclear energy industry.	The Department of Commerce ITA's Civil Nuclear Trade Initiative Accomplishments:
	
	• The TPCC Civil Nuclear Working Group: Regular monthly meetings chaired at the Deputy Assistant Secretary level greatly enhance interagency coordination on trade promotion issues to support the civil nuclear industry.
	
	• Civil Nuclear Trade Advisory Committee (CINTAC): Building off its earlier set of recommendations, the committee submitted supplemental policy recommendations to Secretary Bryson to enhance competitiveness.
	
	• Trade Policy and Promotion Activities of the TPCC Civil Nuclear Working Group:
	
	  – In response to a top recommendation to the Secretary of Commerce made by the CINTAC, the Administration established a new White House Director on Civil Nuclear Energy Policy to ensure alignment of U.S. Government programmatic support for the commercial priorities of the U.S. civil nuclear industry. In addition, the group realigned U.S. Government policy on future civil nuclear bilateral agreements to consider commercial objectives.
	
	  – Developed criteria for prioritizing best-prospect markets and completed a second Top Prospects Market Study to focus U.S. Government resources on top priority markets.
	
	  – Facilitated the Secretary of Commerce's infrastructure development mission to India, the ITA Under Secretary's second policy visit to Central and Eastern Europe, the U.S. industry program at China's nuclear exhibition, and the International Atomic Energy Agency's general conference.
	
	  – Supported joint declarations on nuclear commercial cooperation with Slovakia.
	
	  – Supported the launch of the U.S.-Brazil Strategic Energy Dialogue—a Presidential Initiative.
	
	  – Engaged Japan to ratify a global nuclear liability convention.
	
	  – Supported the Department of Commerce Acting Secretary's visit to Poland for the U.S.-Poland Business Summit and related policy and advocacy meetings.
	
	• Stakeholder Resources:
	
	  – Administered Civil Nuclear Web Portal and Civil Nuclear Exporters Guide (available at www.trade.gov/civilnuclear)
	
	  – Organized educational workshops for industry, which includes an Under Secretary–led financing workshop
	
	• Next Steps:
	
	  – Advance and implement whole-of-government commercial strategy through TPCC Civil Nuclear Working Group in direct coordination with the National Security Council-led Interagency Policy Committee.
	
	  – Establish a public-private partnership with U.S. industry to enhance the global competitiveness of U.S. industry.
	
	  – Develop more accurate and specific data on trade flows and market size.
	
	  – Lead trade missions to best-prospect markets and demonstrate high level-U.S. Government support at major conferences.
	
	  – Pursue Commercial Joint Declarations, MOUs, and Commercial Dialogues.
	
	  – Organize civil nuclear codes and standards workshops in selected markets.
	
	  – Advance global nuclear liability regime, the Convention on Supplemental Compensation.

Short-Term Recommendations:

Recommendation	Status and Next Steps
Leverage the vast capabilities of minority business enterprises in exporting. Design outreach and trade facilitation programs specifically geared to minority business enterprises.	Recommendation: Identify and encourage U.S. minority-owned business enterprises (MBEs) with export potential to enter the global marketplace as well as to help already exporting MBEs become more successful and competitive internationally. According to the 2007 Survey of Business Owners sponsored by the U.S. Census Bureau, MBEs are twice as likely to generate sales through exports compared to non-minority firms because of their unique competitive advantages in the global marketplace, including language skills, proficiency in foreign cultures and business practices, and existing connections with potential local clients. In addition, MBEs are more than three times as likely to have businesses generating 100 percent of all their sales in exports compared to non-minority firms. The TPCC Secretariat is currently assisting the Minority Business Development Agency (MBDA) in determining more effective ways MBDA can support U.S. exports under the NEI, including the possibility of creating a Global Business Unit whose mission is to help MBEs enter, compete, and succeed in the global marketplace. The success and unique leverage MBEs have achieved in exporting has not yet been fully understood or used. In addition to helping MBEs become more active in exporting, TPCC agencies should look into ways to facilitate their joint business ventures with non-minority U.S. firms in global export markets. As part of the Department of Commerce, MBDA is the only federal agency created specifically to foster the growth of minority-owned businesses in America. Potential contributions include the following: (1) connecting both first-time and already exporting MBDA clients to ITA and TPCC agencies, (2) providing access to a nationwide network of 40 MBDA Business Centers for new client outreach and other export promotion activities, (3) helping MBE exporters referred from ITA and other TPCC agencies become more successful and competitive through MBDA programs and resources, and (4) leveraging the current success of MBEs in their home markets to help other MBEs.
Increase the budget for trade-promotion infrastructure.	In FY 2013, the ITA will allocate its resources to priority markets and sectors with the greatest export potential for U.S. companies; it will leverage the Export.gov web platform as part of the larger BusinessUSA.gov platform to provide value added assistance to additional U.S. firms, and it will expand the SelectUSA program to attract and retain foreign direct investment—and jobs—in the United States. To reach these goals, the President's FY 2013 budget seeks $30.3 million to expand the U.S. and Foreign Commercial Service's overseas export promotion activities and $12.3 million to implement the SelectUSA program's mission of promoting business investment in the United States by foreign and domestic sources.

Long-Term Recommendations:

Recommendation	Status and Next Steps
Increase coordination with state government export promotion programs and nonprofit associations.	Metro Export Plans (MEPs): See pp. 12–13 for highlights on the MEP. USTDA's Making Global Local Initiative: See p. 13 for highlights of Making Global Local.
Identify and encourage exports by U.S. companies selling technologies in high-growth sectors.	The EPC has identified a list of priority markets and sectors. The TPCC agencies are preparing detailed action plans to identify key export opportunities and the actions TPCC agencies should take that would have the greatest impact in promoting increased U.S. exports to the priority markets or sectors. This priority-setting initiative has been instrumental in developing coordinated strategic approaches to the U.S. Government's export promotion efforts. The TPCC agencies will execute the action plans by making sure that U.S. Government officials' export promotion related activities can have the greatest impact on increasing U.S. exports. For example, ITA is targeting international trade shows most likely to draw participants from priority markets or related to the priority sectors identified. TPCC agencies are in the process of coordinating their activities to better address the priorities identified. The China-based American Rail Working Group (comprising 37 U.S. companies interested in doing business in China, the Department of Commerce, Department of Transportation's Federal Railway Administration, and China's Ministry of Railways) met monthly in 2011 to exchange information and will continue to do so in 2012.
Increase federal export assistance for U.S. companies exporting to Brazil, India, and China.	The trade promotion agencies are maintaining a high level of commitment to Brazil, India, and China as priority growth markets. For example, over 2011 and 2012, the Department of Commerce is supporting: In Brazil, 12 certified foreign trade shows, 37 foreign buyer delegations to U.S. trade shows, and 12 trade missions, In India, 18 certified foreign trade shows, 19 foreign buyer delegations to U.S. trade shows, and 14 trade missions, In China, 35 certified foreign trade shows, 28 foreign buyer delegations to U.S. trade shows, and 3 trade missions.
Implement an export promotion strategy for designated Next Tier markets.	As discussed earlier, the EPC has identified a list of priority markets and sectors. The TPCC agencies are preparing detailed action plans to identify key export opportunities and the actions TPCC agencies should take that would have the greatest impact in promoting increased U.S. exports to the priority markets or sectors. This priority-setting initiative has been instrumental in developing coordinated strategic approaches to the U.S. Government's export promotion efforts. Additional input from various private-sector stakeholders, including the President's Export Council, has helped identify areas where resources should be focused to have the greatest impact. The TPCC agencies will execute the action plans by making sure that U.S. Government officials' export promotion related activities can have the greatest impact on increasing U.S. exports. For example, ITA is targeting international trade shows most likely to draw participants from priority markets or related to the priority sectors identified. TPCC agencies are in the process of coordinating their activities to better address the priorities identified.

Priority 3: Trade Missions

Trade missions offer a proven, cost-effective tool for U.S. companies to learn firsthand about global markets. By participating in trade missions, U.S. companies can meet one-on-one with foreign government decision makers and business contacts, including potential agents, distributors, and partners. Access to foreign government officials and in-country business contacts can lead to long-term success in those markets. Trade missions receive a great deal of attention from foreign government representatives, business leaders, and media outlets, and provide U.S. companies the prestige of being part of an official U.S. Government trade delegation.

Recommendation	Status and Next Steps
Expand and better target trade missions.	In 2011, the TPCC agencies met their goal of 40 missions and exceeded their 480 participant goal by more than 70 participants, for a total of 40 missions to 22 countries with more than 550 participants. More than 80 percent of companies participating in trade missions in 2011 were SMEs. TPCC agencies focused trade missions on NEI markets and sectors. The missions traveled to many key NEI countries including China, India, South Africa, Brazil, and Saudi Arabia. The U.S. Government also focused trade missions on key sectors where the United States has a competitive edge, such as education, health care, franchising, and energy.
	USDA doubled the number of trade missions to targeted markets in 2011 from two to four. USDA-led trade missions to Indonesia and Vietnam were held in conjunction with USDA-endorsed international trade shows. A USDA-led trade mission to Colombia and Panama was timed just weeks after Congressional approval of FTAs with those countries. USDA also led a trade mission to Peru.
	In support of the NEI, USTDA launched the International Business Partnership Program (IBPP) in a targeted effort to maximize the exports immediately resulting from the Agency's activities. Under the IBPP, USTDA consistently prioritized its resources in reverse trade missions, which bring foreign buyers to the United States pending upcoming procurements to observe the design, manufacture, and operation of U.S. equipment and services that can help them achieve their development goals. In FY 2011 alone, these reverse trade missions connected more than 600 foreign buyers with 1,000 U.S. company representatives located across the country.
Increase the number of trade missions led by senior officials from the EPC and TPCC agencies.	The Department of Commerce had 13 missions led by senior-level officials in 2011. Several planned missions had to be postponed because of the Arab Spring. Then-Secretary Locke led a high-tech multi-sector mission to India and was accompanied by senior officials from Ex-Im Bank and USTDA. Under Secretary of Commerce for International Trade Sánchez led the first NEI service mission in education to Indonesia and Vietnam with more than 70 universities and colleges. Such trade missions receive important planning, information, and logistics support from the multiple agencies and sections that compose the export promotion teams at U.S. diplomatic posts abroad.
	USDA trade missions to target markets were led by Farm and Foreign Agricultural Services Under Secretary Scuse. USDA led 57 different agribusinesses on agricultural trade missions to Peru, Indonesia, Vietnam and Colombia/Panama, resulting in $15 million of reported sales (preliminary data). During the trade missions, participants met with local entrepreneurs for one-on-one business meetings, met host country and U.S. Government officials, and participated in on-site visits.
Expand follow-up with companies participating in trade missions.	Successfully implemented in 2011 (see 2011 NES regarding establishment of new standard operating procedures for company follow-up).
Increase the number of reverse trade missions that bring foreign procurement officials to the United States to meet with U.S. suppliers.	In support of the NEI, USTDA hosted 50 reverse trade missions in FY 2011, exceeding its commitment of 40 reverse trade missions by 25 percent. USTDA's reverse trade missions connected 600 foreign delegates from various developing and middle-income countries to more than 1,000 U.S. company representatives across the country. These carefully planned visits expose key decision makers from abroad to the design, manufacture, and demonstration of U.S. equipment and services pending upcoming procurements in order to position U.S. firms, large and small, to increase their exports to those emerging markets.
	The Department of Transportation's Federal Transit Administration hosted in September 2011 a reverse trade mission from Mumbai, India, that focused on infrastructure, including public transportation. India's rapidly developing transit systems, particularly in megacities such as Mumbai, present myriad opportunities for U.S. firms. The Indian delegation visited Washington, DC; Denver, CO; and San Francisco, CA, and met with U.S. suppliers. One direct result was a $700,000 order for electronic bus information display systems from Tata Motors Ltd, the largest producer of buses in India.
Strengthen the federal export promotion infrastructure to support trade missions.	The President's FY 2013 Budget requested approximately $30.3 million in additional funding to place more Foreign Commercial Service Officers and locally engaged staff members in high-growth markets such as China, India, and Brazil.
Connect U.S.-led trade missions with key trade shows.	The Trade Missions Program regularly looks for opportunities to combine trade missions with trade shows. For example, the FY 2011 Aerospace to China Trade Mission included participation in Airshow China.

Priority 4: Commercial Advocacy

Commercial advocacy[38] is designed to coordinate Federal Government resources and authority to level the playing field on behalf of U.S. business interests as they compete for government-funded projects abroad. This service has grown increasingly vital as market-distorting subsidies and political inducements by foreign governments have altered the competitive landscape in a growing number of markets. Commercial advocacy is especially relevant when U.S. companies compete against state-owned enterprises or other countries' "national champions."[39] The commercial advocacy process leverages the instruments of U.S. diplomacy on behalf of U.S. companies to ensure fairness and transparency. Coordinating export promotion resources on behalf of important export opportunities allows U.S. leadership to highlight the unique advantages of U.S. products and services.

Short-Term Recommendations:

Recommendation	Status and Next Steps
Enhance interagency coordination.	The Advocacy Center has been the focal point for facilitating interagency communication about relevant U.S. officials' trips and meetings with foreign counterparts and for providing background and talking points on key advocacy cases. In 2011, 56 examples of such interagency cooperation were documented.
Promptly bring exceptional commercial advocacy cases to the attention of the White House.	The Advocacy Center regularly communicates with the White House, through the National Security Staff, to discuss what active advocacy cases are appropriate to discuss whenever the President or Vice President is meeting with a Head of State, either when traveling abroad or when a Head of State visits the United States. Furthermore, the White House regularly receives company background and active case materials whenever the President or Vice President travels domestically.
	For example, on a November 2010 trip to Indonesia, President Obama advocated on behalf of Electro-Motive Diesel (EMD; La Grange, IL) on behalf of its efforts to sell 44 locomotives to PT Kereta Api (PTKA), the Indonesian national railway. On August 12, 2011, EMD reported to the Advocacy Center that it had won the procurement, valued at $140 million, with U.S. export content of $94 million. This sale will support or create more than 500 jobs in the United States.
Increase U.S. companies' awareness of the benefits of commercial advocacy.	The Advocacy Center identified five target sectors: SMEs; renewable energy and clean technology, health care, infrastructure, and financial services. From the launch of the NEI to August 31, 2012, the Advocacy Center staff reported participating in more than 200 outreach meetings, many targeting those specific sectors. Most of these meetings included SMEs, and in a few cases, the meetings specifically targeted SMEs for outreach. The Advocacy Center has observed an increase in the business from the energy, health care and infrastructure sectors since the start of 2011 when the Advocacy Center began tracking the number of pending cases for each of those sectors.
	After the announcement of key recommendations in the report on the NEI in September 2010, the number of SME wins increased by 85 percent from FY2010 to FY2011. From FY2010 to FY 2012 (year to date), the Advocacy Center has helped SMEs win 20 procurements. These projects have a total value of $1.4 billion with a U.S. export content of $697 million.
Improve market intelligence on key export opportunities.	In 2012, ITA and the State Department's Commercial and Business Affairs Office launched an effort to more effectively identify, target, promote, and help U.S. companies secure prime and sub-prime contracts. The goal is development of a committed TPCC working group that uses the tools available to the Federal Government working in concert with foreign governments and the private sector (domestically and abroad). A core group of agencies (Commerce, State, Energy, Transportation, USTDA, Ex-Im Bank, OPIC, and SBA) have initially identified nine NEI priority countries (Brazil, Colombia, China, India, Indonesia, Turkey, Qatar, Saudi Arabia, and the United Arab Emirates) where there are substantial infrastructure opportunities (both short term and long term). The plan is to identify specific infrastructure projects in each of those markets and develop a whole-of-government action plan for how the U.S. Government can help U.S. companies know about, and compete for those projects. If successful, the pilot may be expanded to more countries and projects, as well as to longer-term bilateral relationship–building activities.

Long-Term Recommendations:

Recommendation	Status and Next Steps
Develop and deploy interagency commercial advocacy teams focused on key sectors and international markets. Create interagency teams in key sectors that could benefit from stronger commercial advocacy.	Advocacy Center staff members and USEAC teams, specifically Aerospace and Defense and Trade Winds Asia, traveled to principal trade shows to assist with active advocacy cases, network with clients, and meet potential clients. Briefings were made to U.S. company delegations at these events. Other examples include meetings of the TPCC Civil Nuclear Working Group to discuss advocacy. In FY 2011, Advocacy Center principals and regional managers met with their counterparts at the Department of Defense, the Department of Energy, the Department of Transportation, the National Security Council, the Department of State, Ex-Im Bank, and USTDA to expand their number of cases with the Advocacy Center.
Review the impact of trade finance and export credit on commercial advocacy.	Successfully implemented in 2011 (see 2011 NES for Ex-Im Bank training of Advocacy Center staff members).

---

38 For purposes of this report, commercial advocacy, also referred to as trade advocacy, encompasses Federal Government advocacy for export transactions involving commercial and defense articles.

39 In many industries (e.g., nuclear power), state-owned companies and "national champions" are able to leverage the full economic, financial, and diplomatic support of their host country government in the pursuit of major international contracts, thus giving them a distinct advantage compared to U.S. privately-owned competitors.

Priority 5: Increasing Export Financing

Export financing is a crucial part of exporting. Government trade and investment financing agencies, such as Ex-Im Bank and SBA, step in to fill market gaps when the private sector is unable to provide adequate financing to support certain transactions with greater real or perceived risk. Since the global financial crisis, the private sector financing gaps for U.S. exporters has remained wide, with private sector lenders having increased the cost of funds, shortened maturities, or tightened lending standards. U.S. Government trade financing programs can also be critical to leveling the playing field by matching financing provided by foreign governments.

Recommendation	Status and Next Steps
Make more financing available through existing financing platforms and through new products.	In FY 2011, Ex-Im Bank was able to increase the extension of financing, primarily through its existing financing programs, by 33 percent over the prior year and 56 percent over the prior two years to $32.7—$6 billion of which benefited U.S. small businesses. This increase represented more than 3,700 transactions, a 7 percent increase compared to the previous year. The products Ex-Im Bank has launched over the past few years continue to contribute to this total. Ex-Im Bank's Board of Directors has approved four supply chain finance transactions since the Bank launched the program in FY 2010—one was approved in FY 2010, two in FY 2011, and one has been approved thus far in FY 2012. The FY 2011 and FY 2012 transactions make available a combined total of about $1.4 billion of financing annually to U.S.-based suppliers of Caterpillar, Boeing and Navistar—all of which have several thousand small businesses supplying critical components for exports. In response to the requests of exporters and Ex-Im Bank's broker-partners in 2011, Ex-Im Bank added a new product to its flagship Trade Credit Insurance program—Express Insurance. Since the product's inception in mid-FY2011, Ex-Im has issued more than 380 Express Insurance policies (see the 2011 NES for more background on the program). This product will be recognized in the coming year by Harvard University for its innovative approach in solving a problem faced by exporters. Ex-Im Bank also introduced innovative lending products to make more financing available for both short- and long-term lending over the past year. In FY2012, Ex-Im launched the Global Credit Express Pilot Loan Program, which delivers small business short-term working capital loans directly to creditworthy small business exporters. These firms are unable to obtain commercial loans because of high transaction costs faced by banks in underwriting and servicing them. Ex-Im Bank has received 19 applications for this product since the pilot program was initiated in March 2012. Ex-Im Bank is also filling liquidity gaps in long-term funding with its bond product/capital market option, which taps new funding sources by allowing the guaranteed lender to issue bonds against Ex-Im Bank guaranteed loans; this financing option was revitalized in FY2009 and has been actively used over the past several years as liquidity in the private lending community has tightened. Borrowers funded their purchases using Ex-Im Bank's capital market option for 17 transactions worth $2.4 billion in FY 2010, for 5 transactions worth $747 million in FY 2011, and for 4 transactions worth $555 million thus far in FY2012. More than 500 SBA lenders signed up to begin offering loans under the now permanent Export Express program, which demonstrated strong results during its first year: the number of Export Express loans increased by 20.1 percent and the dollar amount of those loans increased by 168%% between FY2010 and FY2011. SBA participated with the President in a major Manufacturing In-Sourcing Forum in January 2012 and promoted the use of the existing International Trade Loan to assist manufacturers in bringing their production and jobs back home. SBA saw a 440 percent increase in the number of loans and a 1,256 percent increase in the dollar amount of those loans between FY2010 and FY2011. SBA expects continued growth in the use of the ITL program as the Administration increases its focus on manufacturing because the program provides small businesses the capital they will need to modernize and expand their plants and the equipment needed to meet international competition and overseas demand. Paralleling the overall growth in U.S. exports, the number of loans under the SBA's Export Working Capital loan program, which is limited to funding export transactions, increased 14.8 percent while the dollar volume of those loans increased 138 percent —a reflection of the new $5 million maximum loan amount now available under this program. Because of the Small Business Jobs Act, SBA was also able to temporarily increase its local presence for offering international trade finance counseling and export financing programs, by expanding its network of export finance specialists from 18 to 20 U.S. Export Assistance Centers (where they share offices with the U.S. Commercial Service and, in some locations, with Ex-Im Bank staff members, as well). USDA's export credit GSM-102 program is capped by law at $5.5 billion and, as a result, no greater financing is available. Because the GSM-102 program is capped, USDA focused on realigning program announcements. In 2011, the GSM-102 export credit guarantee program facilitated the export of approximately $4.1 billion in agricultural products, an increase of 28 percent over 2010 sales. Program activity in 2011 has also increased sales to 11 additional countries compared to 2010, and USDA has received registrations for fish and breeding cattle for the first time in more than six years.
Expand the eligibility criteria for lending to SMEs.	Successfully implemented. See the 2011 NES for Ex-Im Bank and SBA measures to expand eligibility.
Focus lending activities and outreach on priority international markets.	As highlighted in the 2011 NES, Ex-Im Bank is open for business in 175 countries, but has identified nine priority countries with the greatest potential for increasing exports: Brazil, Colombia, Mexico, Nigeria, South Africa, Turkey, India, Indonesia, and Vietnam. The Bank has a team dedicated to these markets and intends to increase its activity in those nine countries by nearly 50 percent from $12.3 billion in FY2011 to $18.5 billion in FY 2012. The projected investment in infrastructure across those countries over the next five years is more than $2 trillion. Increased access to this growing market for products and services will help small and large U.S. exporters in many sectors maintain current employment levels and create a significant number of new jobs. The Bank is implementing outreach plans for each market that include targeted private sector and public sector buyers, financial institutions and government agencies. In FY2011, the Bank surpassed the $1 billion mark for the first time in support of U.S. exports to Sub-Saharan Africa, with almost $1.4 billion authorized for the region, including $937.4 million for South Africa. Ex-Im Bank supported 8 percent of all U.S. exports to Sub-Saharan Africa in 2011. Participating primarily in emerging markets, USDA made the GSM-102 program available in 122 countries and facilitated exports to 35 of those countries in 2011, an increase of 21 percent over the previous year. Eleven of those 35 countries (31 percent) were markets that had not participated in GSM the prior year.

Recommendation	Status and Next Steps
Increase and focus outreach efforts to globally competitive industries and underserved sectors of the economy with incremental export potential.	Ex-Im Bank is focusing on a number of industries with high potential for U.S. export growth: agribusiness, aircraft and avionics, construction, medical technologies, mining, oil and gas, and power generation, including renewable energy. These industries support the critical needs of a growing number of middle-class consumers in emerging and other global markets that offer U.S. exporters some of their best opportunities for sales growth. Accomplishments in FY 2011 include the following: an authorized amount of $1.4 billion to support U.S. telecommunications-related exports, including $1.3 billion for satellites; an approval of more than $1.2 billion in support of U.S. construction equipment and services exports to many foreign projects; an authorized amount of more than $5 billion to support U.S. services exports, including engineering, design, construction, computer software, oil and gas drilling, architecture, transportation services, legal services, training and consulting; and support for U.S. agribusiness through $830 million in authorizations for exports that included agricultural goods and services, including farm equipment, commodities, livestock, chemicals, supplies and services.

Ex-Im Bank has a Congressional mandate to increase its support for renewable energy exports and has tripled its portfolio of renewable energy projects to $330 million in FY 2010 and doubled it to $721 million in FY 2011. The Bank's Environmental Exports Program offers enhancements including terms of up to 18 years for renewable energy projects, up to 30 percent local cost support within the U.S. scope of supply, and capitalization of interest during construction. To date, Ex-Im Bank has authorized a host of transactions using this program. Additionally, Ex-Im Bank is one of the leading financiers of U.S. exports that contribute to the development of solar energy in India. |
| Increase the number and scope of public-private partnerships. | Ex-Im Bank leverages its resources on behalf of small businesses by working with private sector lenders, insurance brokers, and other financial and trade institutions. By fiscal year's end, 113 lenders were enrolled in Ex-Im's Working Capital Guarantee Program and 105 of these lenders had received delegated authority to provide Ex-Im's guarantee for working capital loans without prior approval from the Bank. A total of 12 new lenders were added to the Bank's lenders list, 8 of which received delegated authority in FY 2011. An additional 20 brokers serving small businesses were added to the Bank's roster of 80 active brokers providing Ex-Im's insurance products. The top five small-business brokers accounted for more than $800 million in small-business authorizations. |
| Streamline the application and review process for U.S. exporters, particularly SMEs. | As highlighted in the 2011 NES, Ex-Im Bank has streamlined processes to serve its customers faster. Adding staff members and streamlining processing in the insurance area of the Bank has decreased the average cycle time for all high volume short-term insurance programs; cycle time for short-term multi-buyer and single-buyer programs has decreased by an average of 30 percent from FY2010 to FY2011. These efforts have also steadily increased the percentage of all deals completed in 30 days or less—57 percent, 65 percent, and 80 percent of deals met this target in FY2009, FY2010, and FY2011, respectively.

Additionally, Ex-Im Bank has launched a multi-year Total Enterprise Modernization (TEM) effort to improve its systems and workflow, which will streamline internal processes, simplify customers' interface with the Bank, and greatly improve the information and knowledge flow within the Bank. Ex-Im anticipates that TEM will help Ex-Im align its information resources with its business strategies and investment decisions.

SBA increased the number of Preferred Lenders under its Export Working Capital loan program (EWCP-PLP) from 10 in July of 2010 to 16 in March 2011—a significant 60 percent increase—as more lenders see the benefit of participating in a program that meets the needs of their small business exporting customers. The Small Business Jobs Act provided that lenders who are participating in the Delegated Authority Program of Ex-Im Bank would now be eligible to participate in the EWCP-PLP program. This change has already made a significant impact on the program, because more lenders can now more easily look to both programs for the best customized financing solution for their customers. Working with the district offices of the Federal Reserve Bank and the Office of the Comptroller of the Currency, SBA and Ex-Im Bank will continue to provide training on their export financing programs to community lenders throughout the country during 2012, with the goal of encouraging more lenders to offer these products to their small exporting customers.

USDA's GSM-102 system and application process was developed for and continues to be refined to provide exporters with the speed in review and confirmation that is needed for agriculture commodity trades. The system is entirely web-based—allowing exporters to register, determine fees, and provide shipment data via the web. The GSM-102 system undergoes continuous review and is updated when issues arise.

As a result of the streamlined exporter qualification process, the number of exporters participating in GSM-102 increased 8 percent over the previous year. As a result of queries to exporters, USDA gained valuable information concerning exporter needs and is working to meet those needs. USDA continues to work closely with members of the Farm Credit System through CoBank. The Farm Credit system is a nationwide network with more than 83 independent, customer-owned cooperative lending institutions serving all 50 states and Puerto Rico and services America's farmers, ranchers, and agribusinesses. |

Priority 6: Macroeconomic Rebalancing

The United States has strongly advocated a rebalancing of global demand as an essential part of achieving a strong and long-lasting global economic recovery. Faster domestic demand growth abroad, particularly in countries with trade surpluses, will enable countries with trade deficits to boost their exports and narrow or eliminate their current account deficits. A more balanced global economy will contribute to a more sustainable global recovery.

Recommendation	Status and Next Steps
Short-term objective: sustain and strengthen the global economic recovery.	In addition to U.S. productivity growth and export competitiveness, the most significant determinant of U.S. export growth over the next few years will be the pace of economic growth in the main trading partners of the U.S. In the short term, working to sustain a strong global economic recovery will likely deliver the biggest contribution to U.S. export growth.

In the second half of 2011, global growth and trade each slowed sharply as financial stresses in Europe intensified. That weakness carried over to the first half of 2012. In 2011, the G-20 Leaders focused on the necessary policy adjustments to stimulate a more rapid rebalancing of the global economy. In addition, the G-20 Leaders developed and committed to a policy action plan to stimulate growth and address imbalances. The G-20 is now actively following up on those commitments to ensure that they are fully implemented. A progress report on implementation was reviewed by Leaders in Los Cabos, Mexico, in June 2012. An Accountability Assessment Framework to track implementation of past and future commitments also was agreed; and new commitments were made to bolster the recovery and demand growth in key trading partners. |
| Long-term objective: Rebalance Global Demand. | Over the medium and longer term, the composition of economic growth of U.S. trading partners will be crucial to U.S. export growth. A broad range of countries need to take policy actions that stimulate the pace of domestic demand growth (especially consumption), thereby increasing their demand for imports. Strong, sustainable, and more balanced global growth is crucial to U.S. export growth. |

Priority 7: Reducing Barriers to Trade

An effective trade policy helps create the market opportunities necessary to expand U.S. exports and support additional American jobs. To advance NEI goals, USTR, working with the EPC and other TPCC agencies, is focusing on four areas to improve market access overseas for U.S. manufacturers, farmers, ranchers, and service providers: negotiating new market access, using existing trade agreements and trade policy forums, pursuing robust enforcement, and strengthening the rules-based multilateral trading system. Priority market access negotiations and activities, coupled with vigorous enforcement of U.S. trade agreements and WTO rules, can substantially expand U.S. export opportunities and respond to growing competition from other countries. (Note: More detailed information about trade negotiations, policy dialogues, and compliance and enforcement activities can be found in USTR's 2012 Trade Policy Agenda and 2011 Annual Report [available at http://www.ustr.gov/about-us/press-office/reports-and-publications/2012-1)].)

Negotiate new market access.

Recommendation	Status and Next Steps
Work to ensure that the World Trade Organization (WTO) delivers real results that lead to economic growth and development.	At the December 2011 WTO Ministerial, the United States and other WTO Members effectively agreed to turn the page—acknowledging that the Doha Round is at an impasse and that new approaches are needed that will lead to credible results. Now is the time to craft innovative approaches to the WTO's work as an institution that liberalizes trade and creates and applies meaningful trade rules. The United States is leading the way with its efforts to advance trade facilitation negotiations, expand the Information Technology Agreement, and develop a new plurilateral International Services Agreement, but all major players must do their parts. The United States achieved the successful conclusion of the revision of the WTO Agreement on Government Procurement (GPA) which will present suppliers in the United States with new opportunities to support more American jobs through broader, deeper access to government procurement of goods and services in many partner countries. The revision of the GPA also included a significant improvement of the text of the Agreement by modernizing the text to reflect current procurement practices and clarifying its obligations. The revision was formally adopted in March 2012. It will enter into force when two-thirds of the GPA parties have approved it.
Conclude the Trans-Pacific Partnership (TPP) Agreement.	In November 2011, the United States achieved the broad outlines of an agreement with the current nine participants in the TPP negotiations. President Obama and the leaders of the participating nations urged negotiators to conclude the negotiation as expeditiously as possible. On July 9 and 10, 2012, respectively, USTR notified Congress of its intent to enter into TPP negotiations with Mexico and Canada. This notification triggered a 90-day period during which the Obama Administration consulted with Congress on these new entrants to the TPP negotiations. Mexico and Canada joined the TPP negotiations as of October 2012, following the successful conclusion of the domestic procedures of each of the current TPP countries for addition of new participants. After 14 rounds of negotiations, the TPP countries have made significant progress across the agreement. The current (15th) round of negotiations took place in Auckland, New Zealand on December 3–12, 2012.
Resolve remaining issues with, and seek Congressional approval and implementation of, the pending trade agreements with Korea, Panama, and Colombia.	In 2011, the United States secured Congressional approval of market-opening trade agreements with Korea, Panama, and Colombia. This achievement resulted from the Administration's concerted efforts during the previous two years to take steps that made the agreements better serve American workers and businesses and better reflect American values. The United States–Korea trade agreement entered into force on March 15, 2012. The United States–Colombia Trade Promotion Agreement entered into force on May 15, 2012. The United States–Panama Trade Promotion Agreement entered into force on October 31, 2012.
Create market opportunities for environmental goods and services through tariff reduction, tariff elimination, and other policy initiatives.	In 2012, during Russia's Asia-Pacific Economic Cooperation (APEC) host year, APEC Leaders endorsed an environmentally and commercially meaningful APEC List of Environmental Goods on which, according to their 2011 pledge, they will cut tariffs to 5 percent or less by 2015. In 2011, they also agreed to eliminate and refrain from imposing new local content requirements that distort trade and investment in environmental goods and services. APEC Leaders further agreed to "pursue liberalization of environmental goods and services in the WTO, including by exploring creative and innovative solutions to advance the Doha mandate to reduce and, as appropriate, eliminate tariff and non-tariff barriers to these goods and services." The United States also is seeking to eliminate tariffs on these goods and to remove measures that discriminate against environmental services exporters in the TPP negotiations.
Level the playing field for U.S. companies competing in key emerging markets by concluding bilateral investment treaties (BITs).	BITs: See p. 7 for highlights on the new Model BIT and other BIT initiatives. During the first meeting under the U.S.-Brazil Agreement on Trade and Economic Cooperation (ATEC) in March 2012, the United States and Brazil agreed to establish an Investment Dialogue. Although Brazil indicated it is not in a position to consider a BIT at this time, an Investment Dialogue would provide a forum to address concrete challenges U.S. companies face in investing in each other's markets and mechanisms for enhancing investment promotion.

Use existing trade agreements and trade policy forums.

Recommendation	Status and Next Steps
Strengthen trade policy engagement with major established partners such as Canada, Mexico, Japan, and the EU.	The Administration continues to make progress under the U.S.-Japan Economic Harmonization Initiative (EHI) with respect to expanding market access for a broad range of U.S. goods and services, as well as addressing cross-cutting issues related to Japan's business environment. In January 2012, concrete outcomes were announced in the EHI's Record of Discussions. These outcomes include improvements by Japan regarding transparency and predictability for the import of automobiles that incorporate new, advanced technologies and features not covered by existing regulation; the introduction of new legal protections that enhance the ability of intellectual property rights (IPR) holders to defend their products and services from unauthorized use through technological measures, such as copy and access controls; and the revision of rules to increase the speed, transparency; and predictability of anti-monopoly merger reviews, brining Japan's process into closer alignment with global best practices; and confirmation that American companies do not face foreign equity restrictions specific to offering Internet-enabled ("over-the-top") video services, thereby helping to ensure they are able to offer innovative new services in the Japanese market.
	Also, under the EHI, the United States and Japan agreed on a set of non-binding trade principles for information and communication technology (ICT) services and will promote wide adoption of these principles by other countries to support the global development of ICT services. These principles include Internet and other network-based applications that are critical to innovative e-commerce, Internet search and advertising, cloud computing, and other services. The principles cover a range of topics including regulatory transparency, open access to networks and applications, free flow of information across borders, as well as non-discriminatory treatment of digital products, foreign investment in ICT services, and efficiency in spectrum allocation.
	In December 2011, parties to the WTO GPA reached a landmark agreement to revise the text of the GPA and expand market access coverage for U.S. goods, services, and suppliers, thus ending a 10-year negotiation. The revised agreement will give U.S. suppliers access to more than 150 additional central government procuring entities in EU Member States such as France, Poland, and Sweden as well as expand access to a new procurement opportunities in other GPA parties, including Hong Kong, Israel, Japan, Korea, and Switzerland.
	During the November 28, 2011 U.S.-EU Summit Meeting, President Obama and EU leaders established the High Level Working Group on Jobs and Growth (chaired by U.S. Trade Representative Ron Kirk and EU Trade Commissioner Karel De Gucht) and asked the Working Group to examine a range of options for expanding U.S. trade and investment to support mutually beneficial job creation, growth, and competitiveness. In its June 19, 2012 Interim Report to U.S. and EU leaders, the Working Group said it had reached the "preliminary conclusion" that "a comprehensive agreement that addresses a broad range of bilateral trade and investment policies as well as issues of common concern with respect to third countries would, if achievable, provide the most significant benefit of the various options we have considered." The Working Group further concluded, however, that "further substantive work" would be "required before a more definitive recommendation can be made" on whether to launch comprehensive trade negotiations. The U.S. Government and the European Commission continue to work internally, with domestic stakeholders, with legislators, and with each other to assess potential challenges for a negotiation, with the aim of developing final recommendations.
	The EU agreed to the entry into force in May 2011 of the U.S.-EU Agreement on Cooperation in the Regulation of Civil Aviation Safety. The Department of Transportation's Federal Aviation Administration successfully worked with EU Member States and the European Council to secure this entry into force; the agreement was originally signed in 2008. The agreement enhances cooperation and reduces regulatory redundancies and inefficiencies between the United States and EU in aviation safety activities, such as facilitating timely safety approvals. This enhanced regulatory cooperation will reduce regulatory barriers and encourage increased trade in aviation products and services between the two countries. U.S. exports of aviation products and services to the EU should increase as a result of the entry into force of the agreement.
	The North American Free Trade Agreement (NAFTA) Free Trade Commission (FTC) met on April 3, 2012, in Washington, DC. At the meeting, the FTC called on the relevant NAFTA committees to continue their work to identify areas where unnecessary regulatory differences can be eliminated and to continue to support ongoing bilateral regulatory cooperation initiatives as well as a new trilateral regulatory cooperation initiative announced at the North America Leaders' Summit on April 2, 2012. At the meeting, the NAFTA FTC asked officials to continue their work linking hundreds of SBDCs in the United States and Mexico. At the meeting, Canada committed to reach out to its stakeholders in regard to similar links with Canadian centers supporting small businesses.
	Under the direction of the NAFTA FTC, in May 2011, the United States and Mexico signed a Mutual Recognition Agreement establishing procedures for each country to accept test results from laboratories or testing facilities in the territory of the other country, which complements the mutual recognition that the United States and Canada have had since 2003.
	In 2011 and 2012, the United States and Mexico have continued efforts in the Twenty-First Century Border (21CB) Initiative and the High Level Regulatory Cooperation Council (HLRCC), which were launched by the two countries in 2010. In 2011 and 2012, the United States and Canada have continued efforts in the Beyond the Border (BtB) Initiative and the Regulatory Cooperation Council (RCC), which were launched by those two countries in early 2011. The 21CB and BtB initiatives facilitate U.S. exports to Mexico and Canada by improving infrastructure and procedures at the respective borders. While somewhat similar, the HLRCC and RCC were designed to promote economic growth and job creation, while improving our ability to protect the environment, health, and safety of our citizens. Specifically, the HLRCC and RCC will facilitate trade by aligning certain regulations, which allows U.S. exporters, including small- and medium-size businesses, to comply with fewer rules for goods being sold in both the U.S. and the foreign market. On April 2, 2012, at the North American Leaders Summit, the U.S., Canada and Mexico launched a trilateral regulatory cooperation initiative to align across all three markets certain regulations within each of four areas: vehicle emissions, railroad safety, workplace chemicals, and nanomaterials.
	On July 6, 2011, DOT and Mexico's Transportation Ministry signed an MOU on International Freight Cross-Border Trucking Services that implemented the highest safety standards and opened the door to long-haul trucking between the United States and Mexico. Under a related agreement between USTR and the Mexican Secretariat of Economy, on July 8, 2011 Mexico reduced by 50 percent the retaliatory duties on more than $2 billion of U.S. products such as apples, certain pork products, and personal care goods. On October 21, 2011, Mexico suspended the last of the retaliatory tariffs.
Build on the results of the United States' APEC host year (2011).	In 2012, the United States built on the momentum established during the U.S. APEC host year by working with Russia, as the 2012 APEC host, and other APEC partners to achieve concrete results and meaningful outcomes. APEC Leaders endorsed an environmentally and commercially meaningful APEC List of Environmental Goods on which, according to their 2011 pledge, they will cut tariffs to 5 percent or less by 2015. In addition, they agreed on a Model Transparency Chapter for regional trade agreements and FTAs that will improve transparency and due process in policy making in the region. APEC Leaders also agreed to launch work in 2013 to address the growing proliferation of local content requirements in the region and to develop guidance for economies on how to implement the APEC Leaders' commitment to establish market-driven and non-discriminatory innovation policy. To improve supply chain performance in the region, APEC agreed to implement a more systematic approach to its supply chain work in 2013 that will identify the policies and practices that contribute to well-functioning supply chains, determine where APEC economies can improve their respective policies and practices, and provide targeted capacity building to assist economies in making improvements.
	DOT has secured acceptance within APEC of an initiative to develop a common facilitative approach to general aviation operations, particularly business aircraft operations, that has the potential to increase U.S. aircraft export sales.

Use existing trade agreements and trade policy forums.

Recommendation	Status and Next Steps
Deepen engagement with major emerging markets, such as China, India, and Brazil.	In 2012, through the U.S.-China Joint Commission on Commerce and Trade (JCCT), the United States is pushing China to make progress on formulating open, non-discriminatory economic policies; enhancing IPR protection and enforcement and the treatment of foreign IPR; improving China's investment environment; and addressing U.S. concerns related to government procurement, standards, and agricultural barriers. Already, a number of working groups under the JCCT have held meetings chaired at the deputies and director general levels, including the Industries and Competitiveness Dialogue, Intellectual Property Rights Working Group, Trade and Investment Working Group, the Commercial Law Working Group, and Pharmaceuticals and Medical Devices Subgroup. Additional working group meetings will be held prior to the 2012 JCCT plenary, which is expected to be held in late 2012 in the United States. This year's work will build upon progress made at the 2011 JCCT meeting in Chengdu, China, where steps were taken to move forward in a variety of areas, including IPR enforcement, indigenous innovation, new energy vehicles, and China's strategic emerging industries. On IPR, China agreed to create a high-level leadership structure to institutionalize systemic improvements to its intellectual property enforcement regime and to further enhance efforts to ensure the use of legitimate software. On indigenous innovation, China issued a measure requiring all levels of government to delink indigenous innovation policies from government procurement preferences by December 1, 2011. On new energy vehicles, China committed that it will not mandate technology transfer nor require the establishment of domestic brands in China, and will allow foreign-invested enterprises to be eligible on an equal basis for subsidies and other preferential policies for new energy vehicles with Chinese enterprises. China also assured the United States that it will provide a fair and level playing field for all companies in its strategic emerging sectors. In addition, the Tourism MOU was extended to three more provinces (27 total) amounting to an additional 169 million potential group leisure travelers. In agriculture, China agreed to discuss all beef products in negotiations to restore market access for U.S. beef when previously the Chinese had only agreed to talk about a narrow range of products. Separately, shortly after the United States and China discussed Avian Influenza at the JCCT, China lifted Avian Influenza–related import suspensions on Pennsylvania and Texas, leaving import suspensions in place for Arkansas, Minnesota and Virginia. During the fourth Strategic and Economic Dialogue (S&ED), held in May 2012, in Beijing, China, among other advancements relating to trade and investment, China recognized the importance of increasing sales in China of legitimate IP-intensive products and services; agreed to prioritize trade secrets in its IPR protection policies and increase enforcement in this area; pledged intensive discussions on the implementation of a prior commitment that technology transfer is to be decided by firms independently and not used by the Chinese government as a pre-condition for market access; committed to submit in 2012 a revised comprehensive offer to join the WTO GPA that responds to the requests of WTO members; committed to open up further, including new sectors, to foreign investment; following up on its S&ED III commitment, issued measures that appear to address China's previous commitments on regulatory transparency; agreed to participate in negotiations for new rules on official export financing with the United States and other major exporters; confirmed that it has amended its regulations to allow foreign insurance companies to sell mandatory third party liability auto insurance; committed to allow foreign investors to take up to 40 percent equity stakes in domestic securities joint ventures, going beyond China's WTO commitment of 33 percent, and to shorten the waiting period for securities joint ventures to expand into trading and other essential activities. During 2011, the U.S. Department of Agriculture and China's Ministry of Agriculture also committed to finalizing the framework of a five year strategic plan focused on food security, food safety and sustainable agriculture to build a stronger foundation for critical cooperation in agriculture. That framework was later signed at the February 2012 U.S.-China Agricultural Symposium, held in Des Moines, IA. A new ATEC was signed during President Obama's trip to Brazil in March 2011. The ATEC represents a significant achievement and establishes an effective mechanism for managing the bilateral trade relationship with Brazil. Its establishment will facilitate the expansion of U.S. direct trade and investment relationship on issues including innovation, trade facilitation, agriculture, and technical barriers to trade (TBT). It may also become a foundation for cooperation in other trade fora on issues of mutual concern. The first meeting of the U.S.-Brazil Commission on Economic and Trade Relations, established by the ATEC, was held on March 13, 2012, in Washington, DC. The United States and Brazil agreed to establish a dialogue on investment issues under the ATEC and to explore greater coordination on issues such as cross-border trade in services, IPR and innovation, biotechnology, and SMEs. Under the U.S.-Brazil Commercial Dialogue, the United States has worked to address barriers to remanufactured goods—a high priority for U.S. companies—and is working to deepen cooperation with Brazil on education, including with respect to a key scholarship program that has the potential to attract tens of thousands more Brazilian students to study in the United States. The United States is raising concerns with India about measures taken in several sectors to limit foreign access to the Indian market to develop its domestic manufacturing capacity. The United States is engaging the Government of India on ways to achieve India's goals without creating unnecessary barriers to trade or investment.
Expand trade policy engagement with key emerging markets such as Colombia, Indonesia, Saudi Arabia, South Africa, Turkey, and Vietnam.	During 2011, the Administration worked with the Colombian government to develop an Action Plan related to labor rights, addressing longstanding concerns. The advances under the Action Plan provided the basis for moving forward with Congressional consideration of the U.S.-Colombia Trade Promotion Agreement, which was approved by strong margins in October 2011 and entered into force on May 15, 2012. The Agreement is estimated to increase U.S. exports by more than $1 billion a year, providing new opportunities to U.S. exporters across a broad spectrum of products. In November 2011, ITA launched the U.S.-Indonesia Commercial Dialogue with the Indonesian Coordinating Ministry for Economic Affairs. The first activity under the Dialogue was a December 2011 symposium focused on the World Bank's Ease of Doing Business Index. Follow-up meetings focused on improving Indonesia's investment climate and developing a capacity-building work stream on RE&EE. Under the U.S.-Saudi Arabia TIFA, the United States and Saudi Arabia are working together to pursue various mechanisms for expanding their trade and investment relationship, such as actions to increase the protection and enforcement of IPR, open opportunities for government procurement, and improve stakeholder engagement in the development of standards and regulations. Under the U.S.-South Africa TIFA, the United States is expanding its cooperation with South Africa on many important trade and investment issues to promote job creation, enhance two-way trade, and further grow the two economies. For example, the United States is raising concerns with South Africa about the tariff differential U.S. companies face because of South Africa's preferential arrangements with other countries. The United States is also engaging South Africa on intellectual property issues through regular dialogue and extensive education and training. The United States and Turkey continued engagement under the 2010 Framework for Strategic Economic and Commercial Cooperation initiative, the primary objective of which is the significant enhancement of bilateral trade and investment links. In 2011, the U.S.-Turkey Business Council, established as part of the Framework process, met for the first time and began working to develop a set of joint recommendations that could be shared with both governments. Under the U.S.-Turkey TIFA, the United States and Turkey expanded bilateral cooperation on SME business programs, explored ways to resolve concerns voiced by U.S. pharmaceutical and agricultural biotechnology companies regarding what they view as overly restrictive Turkish import requirements for their products, and launched a bilateral working group of experts on copyright matters. Under the U.S.-Vietnam TIFA, the United States worked intensively throughout the year to address a range of important trade and investment issues. The United States also worked closely with Vietnam in the context of the TPP negotiations to deepen policy engagement in key areas such as labor, IPR, environmental issues, and trade facilitation.

Use existing trade agreements and trade policy forums.

Recommendation	Status and Next Steps
Use bilateral trade policy mechanisms to expand market-opening opportunities.	The U.S. Government is responding to the NEI mandate by working to launch new initiatives, remove trade barriers, and expand exports through an array of trade policy tools, including TIFAs, BITs, Joint Committees on Trade and Investment, and a number of other dialogues and mechanisms.
	In 2011, the United States began discussions with the East African Community (EAC) on a new trade and investment partnership, including the exploration of a regional investment treaty, creation of trade-enhancing agreements in areas such as trade facilitation, and the development of a stronger commercial engagement between the United States and the EAC.
	As noted elsewhere in this appendix, the U.S. Government used many other trade policy mechanisms to expand market-opening opportunities throughout the world. In particular, the U.S. Government in 2011 launched a Middle East and North Africa Trade and Investment Partnership (MENA TIP) initiative in response to the President's call for deepened engagement on economic issues with MENA region countries in the wake of the "Arab Spring" events.
	In 2011 and 2012, the United States and the six other parties to CAFTA-DR agreed to technical amendments to textile and apparel rules-of-origin under the Agreement which will support thousands of jobs in the United States and in the region and benefit the Western Hemisphere textile and apparel supply chain. Under the CAFTA-DR, the United States also worked with the other parties with the support of the Inter-American Development Bank to develop a CAFTA-DR textile sourcing directory to enhance communication and sourcing between buyers and manufacturers in the United States and within the region, thereby encouraging the growing regional textiles trade and assisting producers in the United States and in the region in capitalizing on the opportunities provided in the CAFTA-DR.
	The Department of Commerce used its bilateral dialogue mechanism with Norway to help General Motors overcome a Norwegian tax classification issue that would have potentially limited the sales of the company's European version of the Volt. Overcoming this barrier will help General Motors, and other U.S. auto makers of similar vehicles, to face a more level playing field in the Norwegian market.
	In 2011–2012, the U.S.-Russia Bilateral Presidential Commission's Business Development and Economic Relations Working Group continued to lay a basis for efforts of U.S. companies to position themselves for increased exports to the Russian market once Russia became a Member of the WTO in August 2012. For example, a May 2011 workshop brought together experts from multiple U.S. Government agencies to share U.S. "best practices" in government procurement with a delegation of the Russian Ministry of Economic Development and other Russian government officials working to modernize Russia's procurement system. Targeted trade missions in the first half of 2012 aimed at increasing exports to high-potential sectors of Russia's economy (including exports of automotive components and energy-efficiency technologies) were among the efforts made to improve prospects for American manufacturers to locate new markets in Russia.
	In April 2012, the United States and Brazil signed an exchange of letters committing to endeavor to designate Tennessee Whiskey and Bourbon as distinctive products of the United States and to designate Cachaça as a distinctive product of Brazil. After the U.S. Government issues a final rule with regard to Cachaça, Brazil is then obligated to designate Tennessee Whiskey and Bourbon as distinctive products of the United States within 30 days.
	USTR intensified its TIFA engagement with the 10-nation ASEAN regional group, collectively the 4th largest trading partner of the United States. USTR held consultations throughout 2012 to take stock of progress on initiatives under the TIFA work plan, including trade facilitation, trade finance, trade and environment, and standards. These efforts culminated in a high-level business summit focused on the digital economy, which was held at the ASEAN Economic Ministers Meeting in August 2012.
Address key non-tariff barriers applied to industrial and agricultural goods.	The U.S. Government is committed to identifying and combating unwarranted barriers to U.S. exports. The U.S. Government's efforts to prevent and remove unwarranted foreign barriers serve the President's goal of doubling U.S. exports by the end of 2014.
	The United States achieved some important successes since the publication of last year's report in dismantling sanitary and phytosanitary (SPS) barriers that blocked U.S. agricultural exports. For example, U.S. negotiators removed specific SPS barriers in Japan and Korea for U.S. cherries and citrus, as well as barriers in South Africa and Sri Lanka for apples and seed potatoes. The United States also worked with Kuwait and Taiwan to lift unwarranted restrictions on U.S. exports of poultry and poultry products, and the United States negotiated for full market access for U.S. beef to the United Arab Emirates.
	USTR secured several important additions to the arsenal of tools at its disposal to combat unnecessary trade barriers and made progress on the addition of others, including: passage of FTAs with Korea, Colombia, and Panama that strengthen the ability of the United States to ensure that the standards-related measures these trading partners adopt are transparent and serve legitimate objectives; the creation of new cooperative initiatives related to regulatory and standards issues, in particular through APEC, to promote the use of good regulatory practices across the Asia Pacific region and to prevent governments from creating standards-related barriers to trade in emerging technologies of critical importance to the United States—including in the areas of "smart grid," solar technologies, and commercial green buildings; progress on the negotiation of a modernized TBT chapter in the TPP that will build on and strengthen current TBT disciplines; and successful steps to eliminate or reduce potential foreign technical barriers to U.S. exports, for example by working with Chile to ensure that diesel emissions standards in Chile continue to allow U.S.-manufactured commercial diesel trucks to be sold in the Chilean market.
	USTR, USDA, and other U.S. agencies engaged Philippine officials to resolve market access and standards-related issues affecting U.S. meat and poultry exports. The Unites States and the Philippines signed a customs administration and trade facilitation agreement, with specific commitments on trade facilitation, including simplified customs procedures and transparency of customs administration, which will promote increased bilateral trade.
	USTR, the State Department, and other agencies worked with the Indonesian government to remove barriers to U.S. movie exports.
	More detailed information about trade barriers can be found in USTR's "2012 National Trade Estimates Report on Foreign Trade Barriers," USTR's "2012 Report on Technical Barriers to Trade," and USTR's "2012 Report on Sanitary and Phytosanitary Measures." These reports were created to respond to the concerns of U.S. farmers, ranchers, manufacturers, and workers who confront SPS and TBT trade barriers as they seek to export high-quality American industrial, food, and agricultural products around the world.
	These new tools were developed through increased coordination between USTR and the Departments of State, Labor, Commerce, Agriculture, and other federal agencies to spot and respond more quickly and effectively when U.S. trading partners fail to meet their obligations under trade agreements to which the United States is a party.
	See p. 8 for highlights on ITA's Trade Agreements Compliance Program.

Use existing trade agreements and trade policy forums.

Recommendation	Status and Next Steps
Enhance efforts to address SME export challenges and priorities in the development and implementation of U.S. trade policy.	The U.S. Government is working to address trade barriers that disproportionately impact SMEs and to enhance SME export opportunities through TPP, APEC, existing FTAs, and other trade initiatives.
	In the TPP negotiations, the United States is working with its TPP partners to support the growth and development of SMEs by enhancing their ability to participate in and benefit from the export opportunities created under the Agreement. This includes joint commitments by all TPP Parties to develop and promote web-based information and resources about the TPP Agreement for SMEs, as well as coordination to ensure that SMEs are able to take advantage of the Agreement after it is implemented. SMEs will benefit from increased transparency, predictability, and ambitious and comprehensive access in TPP Partner markets.
	Through APEC, the United States will work to build off of results achieved in 2011 to address top barriers facing small businesses trading in the region, such as by making it easier to access basic customs documentation and to register intellectual property.
	In 2011–2012, the United States and the EU conducted a series of "best practices" exchanges on policies and programs to support SMEs, including their participation in transatlantic commerce. The October 2011 meeting in Washington yielded a plan for further joint work involving new cooperation between the ITA and the Enterprise Europe Network on joint SME trade promotion activities and collaborative efforts to support SME trade. The July 2012 meeting in Rome included a delegation of U.S. small businesses. As a result of the workshops, the United States and the EU intend to conclude an MOU on SME trade promotion cooperation in 2012. The United States will continue to use the SME Best Practices workshops to reduce transatlantic barriers to trade and to cooperate on trade promotion activities for small businesses.
	USTR, along with other TPCC agencies, works through the FTA SME Working Groups under the NAFTA, Peru, and Chile FTAs, as well as the CAFTA-DR, to develop ways to help small businesses take better advantage of the benefits of the agreements and to discuss the expansion of the SBDC network in the Western Hemisphere under the Small Business Network of the Americas announced by the White House in 2012. The Small Business Network of the Americas will link SBDCs and similar SME support centers in the region and diaspora entrepreneurs through on line platforms and business competitions.
	USTR, along with other TPCC agencies, will work through the Korea FTA SME Working Group to develop information and cooperation that can help SMEs take advantage of the agreement.
	Through the MENA TIP initiative, USTR, along with other TPCC agencies, is working to support SMEs and address the trade barriers that they face, and to develop cooperative activities with MENA countries in transition.
	In addition, ITA led an interagency process to redesign and launch STOPfakes.gov, a one-stop-shop for U.S. Government assistance and tools targeting SMEs that are looking for information on obtaining IPR and enforcing their rights overseas. The resources include a self-paced IPR tutorial available in English, French and Spanish, including an intellectual property audit; the ability to report IPR theft to federal law enforcement; a program to obtain a free one-hour consultation with an international intellectual property lawyer; IPR toolkits for foreign countries; and access to IPR materials produced by the European Commission.
	The Department of Commerce's U.S. Patent and Trademark Office, working with SBA, also conducted a review and released a January 2012 report titled "International Patent Protections for Small Businesses" on the challenges small businesses face in obtaining patents in foreign markets.
	The Department of Commerce, ITA's Trade Agreements Compliance Program also works proactively to identify and remove foreign-government-imposed barriers to exports and investments of U.S. companies, with a special focus on SMEs. In 2011, the ITA Trade Agreements Compliance Program initiated 246 foreign trade barrier investigations, with 88 cases (36 percent on behalf of SMEs. For the same time period, the Program closed 91 investigations successfully, with 32 cases (35 percent on behalf of SMEs). An example of such a win was ITA helping EUR Consulting (EUR), a small California-based engineering company, overcome a foreign trade barrier that unfairly excluded the company from competing for a government procurement opportunity in Chile worth $400,000 to which it was guaranteed market access under the U.S.-Chile Free Trade Agreement (FTA). Leveraging the U.S.-Chile FTA, ITA pressed the Chilean government to reconsider EUR's eligibility to compete for this project, and opened the door for future government contracts.
Pursue active engagement in trade capacity building with emerging markets.	U.S. assistance agencies provide related technical assistance and capacity building to support trade preference programs, implementation of trade commitments, and more open markets.
	The United States continues to work closely with developing countries through the WTO Committee on Trade and Development to foster greater integration of developing countries into the rules-based multilateral trading system. The U.S. Agency for International Development (USAID) has helped more than 28 countries to accede to and implement World Trade Organization obligations—facilitating fair trade among countries including many countries in Eastern Europe as well as Vietnam, Cambodia and Nepal. USAID is assisting in the accession process for Afghanistan, Azerbaijan, Bosnia and Herzegovina, Kazakhstan, Liberia, Serbia, Tajikistan and the Lao People's Democratic Republic, among others.
	As noted earlier, ITA launched the U.S. Indonesia Commercial Dialogue with the Indonesian Coordinating Ministry for Economic Affairs and follow-up meetings focused on, among other things, developing a capacity-building work stream on RE&EE.
	USTDA plays a significant role in trade capacity–building activities in emerging markets. Through technical assistance grants, USTDA advances economic growth in partner countries by supporting legal and regulatory reform related to commercial activities and infrastructure development, the establishment of industry standards, and other market-opening activities. These technical assistance programs facilitate favorable business and trade environments for U.S. goods.
	USAID plays a major role in programming and providing trade capacity building assistance in developing countries throughout the world. For example, in 2011, it launched the implementation of the four-year, $120 million African Competitiveness and Trade Expansion Initiative, which provides funding for the African Regional Trade Hubs located in Ghana, Botswana, and Kenya. The Hubs promote increased trade between sub-Saharan African countries and the United States. Among other things, these Hubs manage activities to expedite shipping through selected trade corridors. In other countries, like Vietnam and Indonesia, USAID is helping governments build institutional capacity so that they may more fully honor and abide by their obligations under international trade agreements.
	USAID also plays a major role in fostering a national operating environment that encourages competition and a level playing field—essential factors to growing enterprises and economies capable of of trading with and purchasing U.S. goods, respectively. Over the past several years, USAID assistance in improving the business environment (as measured by the World Bank's Doing Business report) has played a lead role in supporting reforms in well over half of the top annual performers including Morocco, Moldova, Macedonia, Armenia and Colombia in 2012 and Kazakhstan, Rwanda, Peru, Vietnam and Tajikistan in 2011. Assistance was provided to eight of the ten top reformers in 2010.

Pursue robust enforcement.

Recommendation	Status and Next Steps
Strengthen monitoring and enforcement.	U.S. enforcement successes in 2011 include obtaining a WTO ruling against discriminatory excise taxes imposed by the Philippines on distilled spirits; obtaining a ruling against EU subsidies in the Airbus case, the largest trade case ever heard by the WTO; challenging China's imposition of antidumping and countervailing duties against U.S. exports by requesting WTO consultations regarding Broiler Products and requesting a WTO panel regarding Grain-Oriented Electrical Steel; requesting establishment of a WTO panel after consultations with China did not resolve U.S. concerns regarding China's restrictions on foreign suppliers of electronic payment services (EPS) for card-based transactions; ensuring EU compliance with a WTO ruling to reduce tariffs on information technology products; and requesting arbitration with Canada under the Softwood Lumber Agreement challenging apparent benefits given to British Columbia lumber producers.
	In his State of the Union Address, the President called for increased efforts to investigate unfair trading practices in countries around the world, including creation of a new trade enforcement unit. On February 28, 2012, the President signed Executive Order 13601, establishing the Interagency Trade Enforcement Center, or ITEC. The ITEC is intended to level the playing field for American workers and businesses by bringing a more aggressive "whole-of-government" approach to addressing unfair trade practices, and it will significantly enhance the Government's capabilities to challenge unfair trade practices around the world. The ITEC will increase efforts devoted to trade enforcement, as well as leverage existing resources more efficiently across the Administration. Personnel from various contributing Government agencies will comprise a deep pool of analytical support for trade enforcement efforts, including trade litigators; language-proficient researchers; subject matter and economic analysts; and foreign-based personnel. As such, the ITEC will serve as the primary forum within the Federal Government for executive departments and agencies to coordinate enforcement of international and domestic trade rules. These efforts will include, as appropriate, an increase in engagement with foreign trade partners through the WTO, as well as through use of domestic trade enforcement authorities when necessary.
	For many years, the United States has been aggressively pursuing market access in India for U.S. products such as dairy, poultry, pork, pet food and barley. Presently the United States has very little access because of non-tariff barriers for these and other agricultural products. Over the past two years, the United States has initiated numerous technical and high-level policy discussions with its Indian counterparts to this end, including during the President's visit in November 2010. In addition, USDA and USTR decided jointly to pursue enforcement options under the WTO. On March 6, 2012, the U.S. Government requested consultations with the Government of India under WTO dispute settlement provisions concerning India's prohibition on imports of U.S. poultry meat and eggs. India claims that this trade ban is aimed at preventing avian influenza, but has not provided scientific evidence in line with international standards.
	The U.S. Government advocated on behalf of U.S. exporters subject to foreign trade remedy actions (antidumping, countervailing duty, or safeguard). In 2011, the U.S. Government assisted more than 100 companies, employing more than 1.2 million U.S. workers, whose exports were subject to foreign trade remedy actions involving more than $9.5 billion in U.S. exports. ITA's efforts in this regard helped bring about the successful termination of 13 foreign-trade remedy measures in 2011, resulting in almost $330 million in export markets preserved for U.S. businesses and workers. The United States also continues its robust enforcement of U.S. trade laws with regard to imports and their impact on U.S. industry. At the end of 2011, the United States had approximately 288 antidumping and countervailing duty orders in place, covering more than 120 products from 38 countries.
Redouble efforts to rigorously monitor and enforce existing FTAs.	ITA, through its Trade Agreements Compliance Program, works to monitor the trade agreements to which the United States is party in order to ensure that their provisions are being upheld, and that U.S. companies, workers, and investors are receiving the rights guaranteed to them. ITA monitors the operation of U.S. in-force commercial agreements, both multilateral (WTO) and bilateral, and is also making a special effort to develop robust monitoring plans for the new Korea, Colombia, and Panama trade agreements. An example of ITA's efforts to make trade agreements work was when, on behalf of Minnesota company 3M, ITA successfully convinced El Salvador to ensure a transparent and discrimination-free bidding process for a national license plate procurement worth $5.5 million.
	USTR led annual reviews of each of the existing U.S. FTAs, reviewing implementation of all commitments under the agreement and seeking to address any issues that have emerged.
	USTR will continue to seek to address Guatemala's apparent failure to effectively enforce its labor laws as part of the first labor case the United States has ever brought under a trade agreement. The Administration broke new ground last year when it requested the establishment of an arbitral panel pursuant to the CAFTA-DR for Guatemala's apparent failure to effectively enforce its labor laws.
Use trade-policy tools to seek strong protection and enforcement of IPR.	See p. 11 for highlights on U.S. IPR.
Address corruption through trade agreements and capacity building.	The United States has presented additional proposals in the TPP to strengthen transparency obligations and anticorruption provisions applicable to public officials. These provisions are augmented by U.S. proposals for transparency and due process in customs operations (trade facilitation) and government procurement.
	In addition, the United States achieved strong provisions to increase regulatory transparency as well as provisions to guard against corruption of public officials in the Colombia, Korea, and Panama trade agreements.
	The United States continues to address corruption in numerous international fora, including in the Organization for Economic Cooperation and Development, where the U.S. Government has sought to ensure that U.S. trading partners implement and enforce their obligations to criminalize foreign bribery under the Convention on Combatting Bribery of Foreign Public Officials in International Business Transactions, as well as in the United Nations, under the United Nations Convention Against Corruption, and other regional anticorruption initiatives such as in the Organization of American States, G20, and G8.
	In the WTO, the revised GPA, agreed to in December 2011 and formally approved in March 2012, contains stronger transparency provisions that will also help combat corruption in the conduct of international trade. In addition, the United States and its allies continue to make steady progress in broadening support for transparency and due process in customs transactions in WTO negotiations on trade facilitation. At the November 2011 G-20 Summit, participating countries committed to enacting relevant whistleblower protection legislation by the end of 2012.
	The United States, through the APEC SME Working Group, addressed the trade barrier of corruption in 2011 by establishing three sets of voluntary ethics principles for the medical device, construction, and biopharmaceutical sectors. The next phase of the project over the next several years will be to turn the ethics principles into national industry codes, and conduct programs to train the trainer to geometrically expand the number of local ethics trainers, by sector, across APEC.
	In addition, The Department of Commerce and partners helped launch a pilot African Business Ethics Initiative in Botswana that helped sensitize the country's private sector and government on business ethics issues, and resulted in 13 companies endorsing a Private Sector Code of Conduct that the Government of Botswana had developed beforehand.

Strengthen the rules-based multilateral trading system.

Recommendation	Status and Next Steps
Continue the U.S. leadership role in the WTO's day-to-day activities.	Through its active participation in all aspects of the WTO's substantive, negotiating, dispute settlement, and analytical functions, the United States continues to exercise unique leadership on behalf of the multilateral rules-based trading system. For example, in the WTO trade facilitation negotiations, the United States is a leading advocate for simplifying WTO Members' customs procedures related to the importation and exportation of goods and for making these procedures more predictable and transparent for U.S. traders.
Support Russia's and other countries' accessions to the WTO, obtaining new commitments and market access for American exporters.	WTO members took a major step in December 2011 towards expanding the global reach of the WTO when they welcomed the completion of accession negotiations with Russia, Montenegro, Samoa and Vanuatu. These four countries were invited to complete their own domestic ratification processes and deposit instruments of acceptance to become full WTO Members. During the accession process, all four incorporated WTO disciplines into their laws and regulations and made trade liberalizing commitments, inter alia, on U.S. priority goods and services that will come into force when they become Members.
	In addition, substantial progress was made in accession negotiations with Serbia, Yemen, Laos, and Kazakhstan, and the completion of these accession processes in 2013 is contemplated.
	Russia: See p. 7 for highlights on Russia's WTO accession.
Continue to strengthen U.S. efforts in the standing committees of the WTO.	The United States continues to make maximum use of the WTO's committee structures as a front line mechanism to press for concrete action to dismantle non-tariff and other barriers negatively affecting U.S. exports. For example, in the past year, the United States, in collaboration with a number of WTO members, has raised Argentina's burdensome import licensing regime and other import restrictions in the WTO Import Licensing Committee, as well as the Council on Trade in Goods and the WTO Committee on Agriculture; used the WTO TBT Committee to address India's lack of transparency in its development of technical regulations. In the WTO Subsidies Committee, the United States filed the first ever counter-notifications—more than 200 for China and 50 for India—and proposed improvements to strengthen notification review procedures in the Committee. The United States raised Egypt's import ban on cotton in the WTO Committee on Agriculture that helped lead to Egypt lifting the ban.

Priority 8: Export Promotion of Services

The Federal Government should design and implement specific advocacy and trade promotion efforts for services. As the largest component of the U.S. economy, services industries account for nearly 70 percent of U.S. gross domestic product and are the largest drivers of job creation in the United States.

Recommendation	Status and Next Steps
Ensure that there are better data and measurement of the U.S. services economy.	In May 2012, Congressman David Reichert (R-WA) and Congressman Jim McDermott (D-WA) introduced export promotion legislation that included the President's Export Council's proposal and the Obama Administration's initiative to improve services data by permitting the U.S. Census Bureau and the U.S. Bureau of Economic Analysis to share selected confidential business information for statistical purposes. Although previously proposed legislation also included provisions for sharing data between the U.S. Census Bureau and the U.S. Bureau of Labor Statistics, the May 2012 legislation only covers data sharing between the U.S. Census Bureau and the U.S. Bureau of Economic Analysis. Expectations are that this positive bipartisan step will translate into companion legislation in the Senate and potential passage before the 112th Congress adjourns.
Continue to assess and focus on key growth priority sectors and markets to better coordinate export promotion efforts aimed at the services sector.	In FY2011, Ex-Im Bank authorized more than $5 billion to support U.S. services exports, including engineering, design, construction, computer software, oil and gas drilling, architecture, transportation services, legal services, training and consulting.
	In January 2012, the TPCC agencies and the U.S. Census Bureau issued a special edition of the "TradeSource" e-newsletter focused on federal programs that promote services sector exports (see http://www.census.gov/foreign-trade/aes/tradesource_jan2012.pdf). Articles featured (1) U.S. Bureau of Economic Analysis business surveys that inform U.S. industry market research and policy negotiations, (2) Ex-Im Bank financing of U.S. services exports ($8 billion in FY 2011), (3) U.S. Commercial Service's Global Teams that are partly or fully focused on services sectors (e.g., the Education and Travel and Tourism Teams), (3) and services sector contract opportunities through the Millennium Challenge Corporation and the World Bank.
	The U.S. Department of Transportation and the Chinese Ministry of Transport have established a U.S.-China Transportation Forum that includes working groups on new technologies (rail), hazardous materials transport, safety and disaster assistance coordination, urban congestion, and a ports and inland waterways initiative. The 4th U.S.-China Transportation Forum took place from January 10–12, 2012, in St. Louis, MO, and included a U.S. Business Roundtable discussion with U.S. transportation business participation. The Transportation Forum increasingly attracts attendance from the U.S. business community. The 5th U.S.-China Transportation Forum is planned for late 2012 in China.
Eliminate barriers inhibiting the export of U.S. services.	See Priority 7: Reducing Barriers to Trade (pp. 50–56) for multiple examples of services sector new market access.

Appendix B:
Abbreviations List

21CB	Twenty-First Century Border
APEC	Asia-Pacific Economic Cooperation
ATEC	Agreement on Trade and Economic Cooperation
BtB	Beyond the Border
BIT	Bilateral Investment Treaty
CAFTA-DR	Dominican Republic-Central America-United States Free Trade Agreement
CBP	Customs and Border Protection
CINTAC	Civil Nuclear Trade Advisory Committee
CMTS	Committee on Marine Transportation Systems
DOC	U.S. Department of Commerce
DOT	U.S. Department of Transportation
DOT/SLSDC	Department of Transportation/Saint Lawrence Seaway Development Corporation
DSB	Dispute Settlement Body
EAC	East African Community
EDO	Economic Development Organizations
EPC	Export Promotion Cabinet
EPS	electronic payment services
EU	European Union
Ex-Im Bank	Export-Import Bank of the United States
FAS	Foreign Agricultural Service
FDI	foreign direct investment
FMC	Federal Maritime Commission
FTA	free trade agreement
FTC	Free Trade Commission
GBI	Global Buyer Initiative
GDP	gross domestic product
GOES	grain-oriented electrical steel
HLRCC	High Level Regulatory Cooperation Council
IBP	International Buyer Program
IMF	International Monetary Fund
IIWG	Interagency Investment Working Group
IPR	intellectual property rights
ITA	International Trade Administration
ITC	International Trade Commission
ITEC	Interagency Trade Enforcement Center
MBDA	Minority Business Development Agency
MBE	minority-owned business enterprises
MENA	Middle East and North Africa
MEP	Metropolitan Export Plan
MOU	Memorandum of Understanding
NEI	National Export Initiative
NES	National Export Strategy
OECD	Organization for Economic Cooperation and Development
OPIC	Overseas Private Investment Corporation
RE&EE	renewable energy and energy efficiency
RCC	Regulatory Cooperation Council
SBA	Small Business Administration
SBDC	Small Business Development Center
SME	Small and Medium-Sized Enterprise
SPS	sanitary and phytosanitary
SRTG	State Regional Trade Group
TBT	Technical Barriers to Trade
TFC	Trade Fair Certification (Program)
TIGER	Transportation Investment Generating Economic Recovery (grants)
TIP	Trade and Investment Partnership
TIFA	Trade and Investment Framework Agreement
TPCC	Trade Promotion Coordinating Committee
TPP	Trans-Pacific Partnership
USAID	U.S. Agency for International Development
USDA	U.S. Department of Agriculture
USEAC	U.S. Export Assistance Center
USTR	Office of the United States Trade Representative
USTDA	U.S. Trade and Development Agency
WBC	Women's Business Centers
WTO	World Trade Organization

www.ingramcontent.com/pod-product-compliance
Lightning Source LLC
Chambersburg PA
CBHW080441290526
45791CB00008BA/2574